Jaroslav Ira
Jiří Janáč (eds.)

Materializing Identities in Socialist and Post-Socialist Cities

KAROLINUM PRESS
PRAGUE, 2017

KAROLINUM PRESS

Karolinum Press is a publishing department of Charles University

Ovocný trh 560/5, 116 36 Prague 1, Czech Republic

www.karolinum.cz

© Karolinum Press, 2017

© Edited by Jaroslav Ira, Jiří Janáč, 2017

Language supervision by Kathleen Geaney and Peter Kirk Jensen

Photography by Igor Korzun, Boris Chukhovich and Nari Shelekpayev

Layout by Jan Šerých

Set and printed in the Czech Republic by Karolinum Press

First English edition

A catalogue record for this book is available from the National Library of the Czech Republic.

ISBN 978-80-246-3590-3

ISBN 978-80-246-3591-0 (pdf)

The original manuscript was reviewed by Associate Professor Zdeněk Uherek Institute of Sociological Studies, Faculty of Social Sciences, Charles University and Prof. Olga Zinovieva (Faculty of Arts, Lomonosov Moscow State University).

Contents

Preface

Luďa Klusáková

The focus on identification strategies explored in the volume Materializing Identities in Socialist and Post-Socialist Cities brought together
a team of six authors, who studied and worked together the last six years.
The authors are determined to examine not only what was happening in
the cities in post-socialist countries in the last three decades as a result of
their transformation, but they also delve into what had preceded it. We
hope that readers will approach the book with the same curiosity which
we experienced while working on the research with our students. Indeed,
cities and the identification of citizens with their cities and regions have
been present in the research interests of the members as well as of the
students of the Seminar of General and Comparative History since its
very foundation. This is clearly shown in our six collective volumes published by the Karolinum Publishing House in its series AUC Historica et
Philosophica,[1] and in the five volumes published by Edizioni Plus, Pisa
University Publishing House, and focusing on Frontiers and Identities
in its Cliohres.net book series.[2] We were working very closely with a con-
sortium of four universities the last six years within the Erasmus Mun-

1   Luďa Klusáková – Milan Scholz (eds.), *Studia historica* LXI, AUC Philosophica et historica 1
    (2010), Prague: Karolinum 2012; Tim Kirk – Luďa Klusáková (eds.), *Studia historica* LVII,
    AUC Philosophica et Historica 3 (2004), Prague: Karolinum 2009; Luďa Klusáková – Karel
    Kubiš (eds.), *Studia Historica* LVI, AUC Philosophica et Historica 2 (2003), Prague: Karolinum
    2006; Luďa Klusáková (ed.), *Studia historica* LIII, AUC Philosophica et Historica 1 (2000),
    Prague: Karolinum 2004; Luďa Klusáková (ed.), *Studia historica* XLI, AUC Philosophica et
    Historica 1 (1995), Prague: Karolinum 1997.
2   Luďa Klusáková – Martin Moll – Jaroslav Ira – Aladin Larguèche – Eva Kalivodová – Andrew
    Sargent (eds.), *Crossing Frontiers, Resisting Identities*, Edizioni Plus, Pisa: Pisa University Press
    2010; Luďa Klusáková – Laure Teulières (eds.), *Frontiers and Identities. Cities in Regions and Na-
    tions*, Edizioni Plus, Pisa: Pisa University Press 2008; Luďa Klusáková – Steven G. Ellis (eds.),
    Imagining Frontiers, Contesting Identities, Edizioni Plus, Pisa: Pisa University Press 2007; Luďa
    Klusáková – Steven G. Ellis (eds.), *Frontiers and Identities: Exploring the Research Area*, Edizioni

dus Master Programme TEMA Territories – identities and development, having a common study programme and students. The first outcome was a volume co-authored by TEMA alumni and students, bringing together four generations of TEMA scholars sharing an interest in identification processes linked to nation-building, and often staged in cities.[3]

In the present volume, we decided to respond to the challenges of the latest turn in historiography, to the so-called Material Turn, and look more deeply into the materialisation of identities. The volume can stand on its own as a work of a contemporary generation of junior scholars, but, at the same time, it represents a logical continuity in research interests of the Seminar of General and Comparative History. "Materializing Identities" joined the efforts of lecturers, doctoral students and graduates of our TEMA Erasmus Mundus Master Programme. Jaroslav Ira and Jiří Janáč as the leaders of the team inspired the authors to obey a certain coherence in the application of the concept in question. The contribution of Natallia Linitskaya working in Prague and Nari Shelekpayev working in Montreal, both already advanced doctoral students of urban history, is based on their doctoral research. Olga Niutenko and Ivana Nikolovska were, together with Nari, our very first students of the Erasmus Mundus TEMA programme. Together, we experienced and went through the different intellectual challenges stemming from the academic communities of the four universities involved in the programme. The students fully integrated into our debates and thematically inserted into our research project. We can trace the beginnings of these projects in the early 1990s in the analysis of the uneven development, backwardness, and a variety of forms in perceiving otherness. Not only meeting the other, but also neighbouring, exchanging, competing, and conquering the symbols as well as spaces, was taken into account. Research into the inhabitants' identification with places, strongly related to the perception of spaces in the past, preceded our interest in materialising identities in cities. We are convinced that all of the social processes, all important changes in the urban environment, have a spatial and a three dimensional effect sooner or later. They cannot happen haphazardly, as anything that was and is being done in the city was intentional, and, therefore, it has to be understood as conceived and indeed planned.

Plus, Pisa: Pisa University Press 2006; www.cliohres.net keeps all publications in free on-line access of this research network of excellence of the 6th Framework of excellence.

3   Jaroslav Ira – Jan de Jong – Imre Tarafás (eds.), *Identity, Nation, City: Perspectives from the TEMA Network*, Budapest: Atelier 2015.

The volume is divided into seven chapters. It is opened by Jaroslav Ira and Jiří Janáč in a methodological introduction presenting the position of the authors in the research area, and by Natallia Linitskaya through an overview of the state of urban research in socialist and post-socialist cities. The core five empirical chapters show the possibilities of the concept's application. They are conceived as case studies devoted to the old and new capital cities responding to the challenges of post-war reconstruction, or systemic transformations, together with state disintegration, and the formation of new, successor nation-states. Natallia Linitskaya studied the post-1945 reconstruction of Minsk, with a particular focus placed on a Tractor Plant District as desired by new urbanism for new socialist citizens. In his two chapters, Nari Shelekpayev studied the transformation of Almaty and Astana into capital cities of new states, while Ivana Nikolovska analysed the project of rebuilding Skopje. On top of that, Olga Niutenko dealt with the changes in Chisinau and Tiraspol. Albeit the cities were in a variety of situations and perspectives, the authors share a constructivist approach to identification processes, and curiosity about the different identification strategies and their wider impact. The role of actors in promoting the changes in question and of the wider public on the receiving end was, in particular, the focus of the authors. When we read the chapters carefully, we perceive a common vocabulary, understanding of identification, and materiality concepts related to the cities under scrutiny. Materialisation of identities is an issue inviting for a comparative and entangled perspective in research and discussions. We sincerely hope that our volume will become a valuable contribution in this regard.

The authors were trained together, discussed a common reader of theoretical and methodological texts during their studies and research in the field. They were trained through the international and interdisciplinary workshop ambiance of TEMA, while they were benefiting from the Erasmus Mundus mobility support to circulate between Università degli Studi di Catania, Eötvös Loránd University in Budapest, École des hautes études en sciences sociales in Paris, and Charles University in Prague. The volume's editors were their lecturers, supervisors and, last but by no means least, consultants. The authors are grateful to the TEMA Master Programme generously supported by the EACEA under contract number 512013-1-2010-1-HU-ERA MUNDUS-EMMC, while the research was linked to and supported by the Research Framework of Charles University PROGRES Q09 – History – Key for the Understanding of the Global World.

We would like to express our thanks to everybody who helped with the production of the volume, notably to the two reviewers, prof. Olga Zinovieva and prof. Zdeněk Uherek for providing us with invaluable remarks to each chapter and to the volume as a whole, to PhDr. Kathleen Geaney for the English revision of the whole manuscript, and to Mgr. Iva Sokolová who carefully reviewed the manuscript with respect to the formal aspects. We would also like to thank PhDr. Ondřej Vojtěchovský, Ph.D. and Mgr. Stephen White for their help with particular chapters.

Materializing Identities in Socialist and Post-Socialist Cities

Jiří Janáč – Jaroslav Ira

Introduction

When red tractors paraded on the main avenue of post-war Minsk in the early 1950s, it was not a simple demonstration of achievements by the local manufacturer. The scene was loaded with meanings – the products of a brand new factory, red tractors carried the name Belarus, thus symbolizing the modernization of the Belorussian nation. The parade was staged on a street built in the architectural style of socialist realism and named after Stalin, thus passing on the message that it was Soviet power that fuelled the uplifting of the Belorussian nation as part of the happy community of Soviet/socialist people. The parade in a way crowned the post-war reconstruction of the city destroyed during the Second World War. The former provincial centre had been transformed into the capital of a Soviet republic, modelled after other Soviet cities. Red tractors represented the transformation of the merchant town into a socialist industrial city – a tractor factory and housing for its workers occupied the central position in the new, Sovietised Minsk. In the eyes of observers, the parade blended socialism, the nation and the cityscape of the new Minsk into a symbolic fulfilment of a Sovietised version of Belorussian national aspirations.[4] Red Belarus tractors rolling along Stalin Avenue symbolized the materialization of the Sovietised Belorussian national identity in the built-up environment of Minsk, following exactly the famous principle of Stalin's imperial policy: "national in form, socialist in content."[5]

---

4   See the chapter on post-war reconstruction of Minsk by Natallia Linitskaya in this volume.
5   Martin Mevius, *The Communist Quest for National Legitimacy in Europe, 1918–1989*, London: Routledge 2010, p. 125.

However, from the perspective of this volume, the story of post-war Minsk represents merely an overture, a prelude to another, more recent transformation – the reconfiguration of the complex dynamics between nation-building, communism, and the urban-built environment which took place in the formerly socialist countries after 1989. The identity and meanings inscribed by socialist planners into the urban forms and structures of socialist cities, the messages embedded in the design and memory of Minsk's Stalin Avenue, were suddenly seen as obsolete and obtrusive under the changed circumstances of the political, social and economic context.

The collapse of the Soviet communist project was marked by a wave of nationalism which resulted in the disintegration not only of the USSR, but also of Yugoslavia and Czechoslovakia. After 1989, socialist monuments were taken down and replaced with statues representing the new national narrative – for instance, a new monument celebrating the nomadic traditions of the Kazakh nation complemented the otherwise socialist architecture of the former Brezhnev Square in the Kazakh capital, Almaty, in 1997. Almaty, and virtually every city in the region, experienced a vast re-naming of streets, which, instead of the heroes of international communism, celebrated important figures from Kazakh national history.

Figure 1.1 Main entrance of the Minsk Tractor Plant, 2015.
Source: Wikimedia Commons.

However, the nationalization of the urban fabric was not a simple straightforward process – material structures resisted blunt re-interpretation. Meanings, memories and identities inscribed in the material fabric of the city could not be easily erased and re-written. Despite the complex reconstruction of its main square (including the installation of the national memorial) in the first half of the 1990s, Almaty lost its status as national capital in favour of Astana in 1997. Undoubtedly, the identity of Almaty as the socialist centre of the Kazakh Soviet Republic, firmly encoded in the urban built environment, contributed to the decision to build a brand new capital, detached from history – in a way not dissimilar to the socialist construction of Minsk some half a century earlier.[6]

These two stories represent the main theme of this volume (and both are described in great detail in its empirical chapters), which examines the interactions between the parallel processes of the (re-)articulation of the national myth and the transformation of the urban space in the wake of the transition to global (neo)liberal capitalism. We focus on one specific facet of such post transformation – the materialization of national identities in the urban fabric – or, in other words, perhaps more in compliance with urban studies vocabulary, on the nationalization of post-socialist urban space.

While many if not all cities in the former eastern bloc struggled to reconfigure their urban memory after 1989, we decided to focus solely on capital cities which represent privileged sites of change. Not only that the "post-socialist landscape-swap" was "most clearly visible in large cities and metropolises,"[7] as the national governments could arguably afford far-reaching reconstructions of urban built environments, far beyond the means of a mere municipality, but centres of former Soviet (or Yugoslav) republics also turned into fully-fledged national metropolis overnight, historically, and above all mythically, central places of the new nations and nation states. They underwent massive reconstruction both on the physical and the symbolic level, becoming simultaneously globalized and nationalized. The dynamics behind such transformation was framed by the nationalist discourse which aspired to turn the whole city into a national symbol.

Starting from the assumption that the engineering (planning and development) of the new, modern, globalized national centres intertwined with rearticulating the national narrative, we argue that the urban space

---

6   See the chapter on post-socialist Kazakh capitals by Nari Shelekpayev in this volume.
7   Mariusz Czepczyński, *Cultural Landscapes of Post-Socialist Cities: Representation of Powers and Needs*, Aldershot: Ashgate 2008, p. 109.

of post-socialist capitals can be seen as an arena in which often differing and uncertain (fluid) ideas and visions of the (imagined) nation have been negotiated in close interaction with the memory and the identity of its constructed environment. In doing so, we built on, but also go beyond the traditional culturalist perspective which has dominated the field of urban studies since the cultural turn.

Such an approach treats urban experiences and forms as more or less a passive stage, as dematerialized symbols and texts, and tends to understand their physical form as an expression of political values. Indeed, at least since Schorske's classic account of the proliferation of liberal ideas into the architecture of *fin de siècle* Vienna it is generally accepted that a built environment is, even unintentionally, a physical materialization of the values, ideas and power relations of the given era, and that architecture conveys meanings that designers, set within the broader network of power relations, inscribed in the physical structures.[8] Thus, the materiality of the city is discursively interpreted and imagined rather than "physically experienced"[9] and the city remains "the state of mind" and its material features function as hardly more than "background, arena, outcome, medium, obstacle, text or symbols."[10]

From such a perspective, "post-socialist urban transformation" has been described in literature from various angles as a major discontinuity. For instance Molnár has recently argued that central European socialist cities were "politically mobilized in the service of social change, first in socialist modernization and then in the post-socialist transition."[11] However, without denying the profound impact of such transformation, it seems that rather than an abrupt change, it should be described in terms of a contested and continuous process with specific internal dynamics. Rendering architecture and the built environment as a cultural practice whereby the state is "both materially produced and represented?"[12], as Molnár did, obscures various path-dependencies and continuities. As it seems, urban structures sometimes retain their specific ideological content in spite of regime change and act as carriers of memory and alterna-

---

8 Carl E. Schorske, *Fin-de-siècle Vienna: Politics and Culture*, New York: Knopf 1979.
9 Chris Otter, "Locating Matter: The Place of Materiality in Urban History," *Material Powers: Cultural Studies, History and the Material Turn*, Tony Bennett – Patrick Joyce (eds.), London – New York: Routledge 2010, pp. 38–59, here pp. 39–43.
10 Ibid., p. 43.
11 Virág Molnár, *Building the State: Architecture, Politics, and State Formation in Postwar Central Europe*, London – New York: Routledge 2013, p. 3.
12 Ibid., p. 9.

tive identity narratives. Are not the state and its official interpretation of history simultaneously opposed and contested by material urban space?

We think that the urban space of post-socialist capitals can be seen as an arena in which often differing and uncertain (fluid) ideas and visions of the (imagined) nation have been negotiated in close interaction with the memory and the identity of its constructed environment. While many cities struggled to reconfigure their urban memory after 1989 – some turned to medieval times, etc.,[13] capital cities adopted the identity of the national centre – and, in reaction, the official national history narrative was re-formulated (at least partly) in line with the material memory of the capital.

In this respect, it is important to note that the post-socialist (or rather post-Soviet) nation building seems to contradict, at least to a certain extent, the traditional vision of "eastern" nation-to-state nationalism as the opposite to the western state-to-nation trajectory.[14] The development in (post-)socialist capitals discussed in the volume seems to follow the western example – in the cases of Transnistria, Moldova, Kazakhstan and, to a lesser extent, also Belarus and Macedonia. The persisting urban memory of the capital apparently played an important part in the re-articulation of the national myth in such state-to-nation legitimation processes – either as a straw man, or as a symbol of national modernization. The resulting materialization of national identity in the urban space and its actual content thus reflected meanings and memories imbued in pre-existing physical structures. In the history of technology, this is often described as mutual co-construction of the material and the social.[15]

To conclude, this volume intends to create a small contribution to the growing literature on post-socialist urban transformation and examines the contested process of inscription of the national narrative in the urban environment. Contributors focused on a specific dynamic between socialist urban forms and national identity, thus overcoming the reductive understanding of nationalization of urban space in terms of a one-way imposition of the ready-made national narrative. Before such an examination is developed, the task of this introduction is to provide a basic

---

13 John Czaplicka – Gelazis Nida – A. Ruble Blair (eds.), *Cities after the Fall of Communism: Reshaping Cultural Landscapes and European Identity*, Washington, DC, Baltimore: Woodrow Wilson Center Press, Johns Hopkins University Press 2009.

14 Anthony D. Smith, *Nationalism and Modernism: A Critical Survey of Recent Theories of Nations and Nationalism*, London: Routledge 1998, p. 74.

15 Mikael Hård – Thomas J. Misa (eds.), *Urban Machinery: Inside Modern European Cities*, Cambridge, Mass: MIT Press 2010.

conceptual framework for the study of post-socialist urban space, memory and national identity.

Materialized Memory of Socialism

Post-socialist transitions (under various names) have been studied from different perspectives on a variety of objects. The intensely dramatic alteration of political, economic and social relations has inspired scholarly interest across disciplines. Having been analysed from various angles, the transformation has been repeatedly described as an extremely complex phenomenon that comprised several mutually interwoven processes of economic, political, social and cultural change.

Urban areas became a privileged site for inquiry. Since 1989, sociologists, geographers and anthropologists have compiled an extensive body of knowledge about the complex transformations of urban space in Eastern European and Central Asian countries after the collapse of communism in 1989. The massive and to a certain extent uniform impact of globalization and capitalism on cityscapes (suburbanization, but also skyscrapers) across the former socialist Eurasia served as an invitation for researchers to study such "transition-zones" in more detail, focusing on the dynamic between the transnational forces of capitalism and globalization on the one hand and the local social, cultural and economic context on the other hand. During a complex and often contested transition, urban areas remained centres of economic activity and economic growth, cultural hubs and critical sites for the implementation of innovations. On the other hand, they also witnessed rising social segregation and increasing poverty. The bulk of the literature has been dominated by investigation and analyses of patterns of spatial transformation of urban forms and their economic context.[16]

This wide interest was motivated by the premise that socialist cities were different from western ones. As Czepczyński argues, "Post-socialist cities are post-socialist not because they are better or worse than other cities; they are post-socialist in the sense that they are different from

---

16 Kubeš offers a summary of major articles on European post-socialist cities published between 1990–2012 (over 180 in the high-profile journals). Jan Kubeš, "European post-socialist cities and their near hinterland in intra-urban geography literature," *Bulletin of Geography. Socio-economic Series 19*, Daniela Szymańska – Jadwiga Biegańska (eds.), Toruń: Nicolaus Copernicus University Press 2013, p. 19–43.

other cities."[17] From a cultural geographic perspective, such uniqueness resides in five historically developed attributes of the socialist urban landscape: overall spatial articulation (socialist cities are more compact), spatial scale (the grand scale of civic/public spaces, etc.), spatial organization (large public spaces), land-use balance (lack of functional diversity), and aesthetic ambiance (repetitive and bleak modernist buildings). The post-socialist change, then, is evident "(a) in spatial articulation – suburban growth and blurring of the urban edge; (b) in spatial scale – decreased development marked by diminished spatial and building scale; (c) in spatial organization – privatization of space; (d) in land-use balance – commercialization; and (e) in aesthetic character – pluralization of styles."[18]

As Natallia Linitskaya shows in her chapter, these unique characteristics have been recently studied also from a historical, rather than a geographical perspective. As she concludes, the modernist conception of housing and urbanism inspired urban planning on both sides of the iron curtain to a similar extent, but economic incentives (state-owned land) and the dysfunctional institutional set-up of the command-economy together with ideological imperatives created a unique socialist cityscape. Socialist planners embraced modernist thought about the ordering of space and people through the physical transformation of the constructed environment and aspired at establishing new form of social relations which would in turn "produce a new consciousness."[19] Thus, urbanization could be seen as a key factor in the production of the new, socialist society. In effect, socialist urban forms, even if seemingly stripped of all symbolic content, retain political meaning and significance embedded in their physical, material structure.

Over the years, socialist urbanism, a material expression of the ideas and values of socialism, became an integral part of the urban memory of the city. The city, through its various architectural styles, urbanist vision, etc., forms a specific site of memory in itself. It seems appropriate to argue that a "city remembers" through its buildings, its material development, which to a certain extent recorded the past and materialized the

17 Czepczyński 2008, p. 181.
18 Sonia Hirt, "Post-Socialist Urban Forms: Notes From Sofia," *Urban Geography* 27, no. 5 (2006), pp. 464–488, here p. 465.
19 David Crowley – Susan E. Reid, "Socialist Spaces: Sites of Everyday Life in the Eastern Bloc," *Socialist Spaces: Sites of Everyday Life in the Eastern Bloc*, David Crowley – Susan E. Reid (eds.), Oxford – New York: Berg 2002, pp. 1–22, here p. 15.

memory of the succession of events.[20] The concept of urban memory is not an anthropomorphism here but indicates a "city as a physical landscape and collection of objects and practices that enable the recollections of the past and that embody the past through traces of the city's sequential building and rebuilding."[21]

Central to such urban memory are, of course, symbolic places, which Pierre Nora calls "lieux de mémoire." Nora argues that the collective memory of communities living in continuity with their past has been eradicated in the context of modernization – and substituted by "lieux de mémoire" – sites of memory: objects (both material and immaterial), which deliberately or not, have become symbolic representations of the collective memory of a given community (local, national, etc.).[22] In an urban context, these reminders, the purpose of which is "to stop time, to block the work of forgetting"[23] take the shape of places of memory (memorials, but also historical buildings and historical institutions such as museums), performative practices (commemorations and rituals) and, last but not least, individual objects, notably commemorative monuments.[24] In socialist cities, these took the shape of memorials devoted to the leaders and heroes of communism, and also of monumental architectural ensembles designed to display the successes and achievements of communism. However, other structures, too, less visible but imbued with meaning and memories acted as carriers of memory in an urban space – the above mentioned urban forms, created deliberately to influence the behaviour of a city's inhabitants. Representative socialist spaces changed in character over time, but retain their ideological content – the centrally positioned government centres and prestigious apartment blocks of the Stalinist period had been replaced since the 1960s with pre-fabricated residential blocks situated on the periphery.

The re-naming of streets and other urban place names, or toponyms, is another way of modifying space and conveying meaning through it – as well as specific architectural style and urban forms and the erection of monuments and memorials, discussed above, the renaming of public spaces forms a third major strategy in the materialization of identity in

20   Aldo Rossi, *The Architecture of the City*, New York: MIT Press 1982.
21   Mark Crinson, *Urban Memory: History and Amnesia in the Modern City*, London: Routledge 2005, p. xii.
22   Pierre Nora, "Between Memory and History: Les Lieux de Mémoire," *Representations* 26 (1989), pp. 7–25.
23   Ibid., p. 19.
24   Ibid., p. 7.

urban structure. As Alderman claims, "place names create a material and symbolic order that allows dominant groups to impose certain meanings into the landscape and hence control the attachment of symbolic identity to people and places."[25] Scholars ranging from linguists to geographers to anthropologists have recently refocused their research on the political and identity-making power of toponymy.[26] In this volume, the issue is studied especially in the case of Kazakh capitals and Transnistria.

Nationalizing Post-Socialist Capitals

A relatively significant share of literature on post-socialist cities addressed the problem from the cultural perspective, focusing on the changing meaning of place and space.[27] The reconfiguration of urban space in conjunction with a reimagining of identity has become a popular topic in studies of post-socialist urbanism.[28] The change of meaning, in terms of semiotics we can speak of it as re-signification, took the shape of the renaming of streets and buildings, and also of pulling down socialist statues, etc.[29] It has been recognized that spatial transformations were accompanied by corresponding changes on the symbolic and representative level, characterized in the Eastern European context most notably by the so-called *Post-Communist Landscape Cleansing*, i.e., efforts aimed at the complete eradication of the memory of socialism from urban space – which concerned various symbolic signifiers and sites of memory, such as street names, statues and memorials, and also public spaces and individual buildings and blocks.[30]

25 Derek Alderman, "Place, Naming, and the Interpretation of Cultural Landscapes," *The Ashgate Research Companion to Heritage and Identity*, Brian Graham – Peter Howard (eds.), Burlington: Ashgate 2008, p. 208.

26 Reuben Rose-Redwood – Derek Alderman – Maoz Azaryahu, "Geographies of Toponymic Inscription: New Directions in Critical Place-Name Studies," *Progress in Human Geography* 34, no. 4 (2010), pp. 453–470.

27 See for instance the special issue of *The Geographical Journal* 165, no. 2, *The Changing Meaning of Place in Post-Socialist Eastern Europe: Commodification, Perception and Environment* (1999).

28 See for instance: Kiril Stanilov, *The Post-Socialist City: Urban Form and Space Transformations in Central and Eastern Europe after Socialism*, Dordrecht: Springer Verlag 2007; Czaplicka et al. 2009; and the special issue of *Nationalities Papers* 41, no. 4, *From Socialist to Postsocialist Cities* (2013).

29 Katherine Verdery, *The Political Lives of Dead Bodies: Reburial and Postsocialist Change*, New York: Columbia University Press 1999, p. 39–40.

30 Czepczyński 2008, p. 109.

The memory of socialism has been replaced by a new narrative, predominantly shaped by discourses of national identity. Some authors even argue that the eradication of the socialist past was a result of the nationalization of urban space, rather than a consequence of the transition to capitalism.[31] Naturally, such developments have been most pronounced and visible in capitals, and especially in the capitals of new independent states, the successors of former Yugoslavia, Czechoslovakia and above all the USSR. There were, of course, important differences reflecting different stages and forms of development of national identities and their representation in urban space prior to the collapse of communism. Furthermore, different paths of political development created more (authoritative) or less (democratic) favourable environments for reassertions of national identity in the urban landscape. Despite such differences, which influenced its shape (architectural style, etc.) and dimension, the general pattern of nationalization of urban space in the wake of the collapse of communism can be observed across the post-socialist world.

However, certain parts of the material fabric of the city prove hard to integrate and re-interpret in line with the overarching national identity project. The most illustrative example of such conflict (or tension) can be identified in attempts to assign a new meaning to urban forms which embody the principles and values of socialist (Soviet) urbanism. Sometimes socialist identity cannot be easily erased – the best examples have been found in Poland in such cases as the former "new socialist cities" such as Nowa Huta, which had hardly any other symbolic recourse available;[32] some authors examined the struggles over the future of symbolic structures such as the infamous Warsaw Palace of Science.[33] Light and Young stress the persistence of the constructed environment, the cultural landscape, of socialist cities and its resistance to reinterpretation (both symbolic and functional) in the new socio-political context which results in their status of so-called "left-over" liminal spaces – the spaces "in between."[34] The practice of de-communization has been studied in detail by Czepczyński, who identified four basic strategies on how the

---

31 Alexander C. Diener – Joshua Hagen, "From Socialist to Post-Socialist Cities: Narrating the Nation through Urban Space," *Nationalities Papers* 41, no. 4 (2013), pp. 487–514, here p. 489.

32 Rasa Balockaite, "Coping with the Unwanted Past in Planned Socialist Towns: Visaginas, Tychy, and Nowa Huta," *Slovo* 24, no. 1 (2012), pp. 41–57.

33 Andrew H. Dawson, "From Glittering Icon to…," *Geographical Journal* 165, no. 2 (1999), pp. 154–160.

34 Duncan Light – Craig Young, "Reconfiguring Socialist Urban Landscapes: The 'Left-Over' Spaces of State-Socialism in Bucharest," *Journal of Studies and Research in Human Geography* 4, no. 1 (2010), pp. 5–16.

Figure 1.2 Palace of Culture and Science in Warsaw, 2013.
Source: Piotr Drabik, Wikimedia Commons.

meaning of socialist urban space could be harmonized within the new cultural landscape of post-socialist cities. Not surprisingly, this concerns their complete re-writing, removal, renaming, rededication, and reuse.[35]

Analysing the central European context, Young and Kaczmarek concluded that three major strategies have been applied in the reconstruction of identity in regard to the socialist past – de-communization, a return to the pre-socialist golden age, and westernization. De-communization means deconstruction of identities created in the socialist period, characterized by the erasure of socialist signifiers from public space (the renaming of streets, demolishing statutes); a return to the golden age highlights the pre-socialist heritage and constructs a direct link between the present and the given historical period of greatness; westernization simply means the aspiration to be identified as western and modern, again silencing the Cold War history and its remnants.[36]

---

35 Czepczyński 2008, p. 109.
36 Craig Young – Sylvia Kaczmarek, "The Socialist Past and Postsocialist Urban Identity in Central and Eastern Europe: The Case of Lodz, Poland," *European Urban and Regional Studies* 15 (2008), pp. 53–70.

This set of strategies for the re-articulation of urban identity (i.e., a re-branding of socialist cities) to a great extent overlapped with the materialization of national identity in urban space. According to Diener and Hagen we can identify three major themes in respect to the post-socialist nationalization of urban space: 1) preserving, creating or rebuilding historical landmarks, i.e., the reinterpretation of socialist relics in a nationalist context (take down and replace with symbols of heroic national resistance to communism, alignment – the socialist past as a symbol of the common resistance to Nazism, etc.); 2) contested nationalization – expressions of alternative narratives (identities) resisting the hegemonizing inscription of national identity; 3) the blending of the new nationalism with globalization, expressed in "large-scale architectural ensembles."[37] This overlap suggests that the construction of national and urban identity should be seen not only as a parallel, but as a mutually intertwined processes.

Since national identity is a dynamic phenomenon, which develops through the negotiation of meaning in social interaction, the re-definition of its actual content and its materialization in urban space happen

Figure 1.3 Georgi Dimitrov Mausoleum in Sofia, 1969.
Source: Angela Monika Arnold, Wikimedia Commons.

37   Diener and Hagen 2013, p. 489–490.

simultaneously. National narrative interacts with the urban memory of capitals materialized in the urban built environment. Such memory often represents alternative stories to those promoted by the official authorities of the state. According to Maurice Halbwachs, memory binds groups of people together not least by reference to the physical space; on one hand, a group transforms the space to make it correspond more to its image, and, at the same time, it also "adapts itself to certain material things which resist it."[38] The materialization of national identity in post-socialist capitals appears as an emergent outcome of the interplay between the official (state) politics of memory (itself dynamic) and the actual urban memory of these cities.

The complex re-construction and re-creation of the post-socialist metropoles included memorialization of the city (re-branding), and also focused on selected periods of the architectural history of the city with respect to the national history narrative (selective memory). Simultaneously, it included new constructions and creations, aimed at a re-definition of the city as the heart of a nation and thus responding to the need for the national-self-image in a much broader sense than simply memorialization. As Molnár shows in the case of East Berlin, the debate over its future after 1989, framed as a conflict between the European (i.e., historical) and American (i.e., globalized) city reflected the identity and aspirations of the new German elites (or, more precisely, the West German architects who were in charge).[39]

However, it seems that state intervention in the interaction between urban memory and identity projects might lead to unintended consequences – the revenge of history.[40] It has been pointed out, especially concerning the Second World War material but also immaterial heritage and memory that coercive methods fail to create a stable "past" – it will invariably re-surface at some point in the future.[41] Sometimes, the structure itself, its unexpected solidity, mocks the very attempts at the annihilation of the past. When the Dimitrov Mausoleum was finally taken down in 1999, due to miscalculations in preparations for the demolition

---

38 Maurice Halbwachs, *Memoire collective* – quoted in Rossi 1982, p. 130. For English translation see chapter 4: "Space and The Collective Memory," in: Maurice Halbwachs, *The Collective Memory*, New York: Harper & Row 1980.

39 Virág Molnár, "The Cultural Production of Locality: Reclaiming the 'European City' in Post-Wall Berlin," *International Journal of Urban and Regional Research* 34 (2010), pp. 281–309.

40 Tony Judt, "The Past Is Another Country: Myth and Memory in Postwar Europe," *Daedalus* 121, no. 4 (1992), pp. 83–118.

41 John E. Tunbridge – Gregory J. Ashworth, *Dissonant Heritage: The Management of the Past as a Resource in Conflict*, Chichester: J. Wiley 1996.

the underground floor survived, now hidden beneath a municipal garden, as a tangible reminder of the past.[42] The materiality of the urban environment, thus, poses a significant obstacle to (often national) policies "of collective amnesia" and "selective memory and active forgetting."

Case Studies

As regards geographical coverage, all the chapters relate to a space that could perhaps be defined as the (south)eastern fringe of Europe. Yet there should be some qualifications. What is common to all the chapters, is basically the fact that they are focused on that part of the Eurasian continent that used to be the socialist space. The chapters on Minsk, Kazakh capital cities, and Transnistria share another common denominator, as they deal with post-Soviet space, unlike the chapters on Macedonian Skopje and the historiography of the post-socialist cities respectively, which cross the borders of the former USSR and its satellite sphere. The European confines should also be problematized. Kazakhstan belonged to Europe basically in purely political terms – as part of the USSR that was, not without many reservations, accepted as a European state. After the dissolution of the union, Kazakhstan reoriented toward its southern neighbours and became a significant regional player in Central Asia, although in other respects it still keeps affinity with Europe, as is markedly demonstrated for example by its membership in UEFA. Notwithstanding the fact that the Russians themselves have been viewed somewhat ambivalently in terms of belonging to European civilization, it seems that the boundaries of Europe and non-Europe are partly at stake in the rift between the Russian and Kazakh population of the state.

The frontiers of Europe are also in evidence in the case of Skopje and the reconstruction of its city centre. The choice of neo-renaissance and neo-baroque styles that for the Macedonian (or FYROM-ian) leaders represent *quintessentially European* architectonic styles, refers, even if in a bizarre way, to the notorious ambiguity of the Balkans' not-so-complete Europeanness, the stigma that has been developed by Westerners and adopted by local societies, as famously shown by Maria Todorova.[43] Although some authors deconstructed the idea of the "European city" as

---

42   Tania Vladova, "Heritage and the Image of Forgetting: The Mausoleum of Georgi Dimitrov in Sofia," in: *Heritage, Ideology, and Identity in Central and Eastern Europe: Contested Pasts, Contested Presents*, Matthew Rampley (ed.), Woodbridge, Suffolk: Boydell Press 2012, pp. 131–154.

43   Maria Todorova, *Imagining the Balkans*, New York: Oxford University Press 2009.

nothing but a mobilizing idea that does not have its counterpart in any specific form of city,[44] cities have served as particularly strong markers of the European frontier.[45] This explains the furious efforts by national elites to get rid of the Ottoman urban heritage, as was seen after the establishment of nation states in the region and also in the recent eradication of the socialist urban heritage. Both were viewed as signs of deviation from the properly European course of history and had no place in the search for a typically European model of the city.

In terms of chronology, most of the case studies deal with the contemporary, post-socialist period, though they refer to the past at some points. Only the chapter on Minsk deviates from this pattern, as it is interested in the post-war reconstruction and subsequent development of the city from the late 1940s to the early 1960s. Yet most of the chapters, in a way, do touch on an older strata of history: as already indicated above, the past appeared on stage either in the form of myths and national narratives that were constructed in the wake of the transformation and inscribed in the urban fabric or in the form of material, as well as in intangible traces (such as street names) that have formed a contested heritage in the respective cities.

The opening chapter by Natallia Linitskaya presents a detailed overview of the results of research on socialist and post-socialist cities. She uses meetings and conferences of the European Association for Urban History (EAUH) as a lens, or rather a magnifying glass, through which general trends in the conceptualisation of post-socialist cities can be identified. As she points out, the existing literature often builds on ideas of socially constructed space and thus clearly demonstrates the impact of the cultural (and spatial) turn in urban studies. On the one hand, the authors emphasize the importance of social and cultural forces (politics, ideology, and also institutional practices) in the development of the material lay-out of socialist and post-socialist cities in what we might call a from-above perspective. On the other hand, some attention has also been paid to the from-below perspective, which makes visible the manner in which the projections and inscriptions of meaning onto the physical qualities of space were "consumed" – i.e., lived, perceived, and also contested and opposed, by the citizens and the inhabitants of socialist cities.

---

44   Dieter Hassenpflug, *Die europäische Stadt: Mythos und Wirklichkeit*, Hamburg: LIT 2002.

45   Friedrich Lenger – Klaus Tenfelde, *Die europäische Stadt im 20. Jahrhundert: Wahrnehmung – Entwicklung – Erosion*, Köln: Böhlau 2006.

Natallia identifies four particularly rewarding (and popular) research topics in the analysed body of literature. First, she focuses on the question of how the ideological organization of space can be seen as a means of societal "ordering," and how spatial forms translated (or were intended to translate) into the organization and formation of socialist society – how experiencing the ideologically-shaped city turned individuals into members of socialist society. Second, Natallia discusses how communist ideology was translated into material design and underlines the fact that despite various practical problems socialist urbanism (especially socialist housing) successfully fulfilled the ideological goal of representing the idea of common well-being. The failures of socialist urbanism are discussed in the third part. Natallia focuses on the system of the state distribution of housing and demonstrates, using several examples from literature, how such selection and regulation resulted in spatial segregation and inspired the formation of alternative urban identities. The fourth and final part analyses the materialization of memory as a basis for collective identity in urban space. Here, Natallia raises the question of the material obduracy of socialist inscriptions in the urban fabric, concluding that the socialist city, and the ideological imperatives embedded in its structures, continues to influence our present and future.

The second chapter, also authored by Natallia, provides an empirical counterpart to her theoretical and methodological overview. Here she deals with urbanization in Belorussia in the post-war period of high Stalinism and its aftermath. She analyses the symbolic modernization of Belorussia and argues that the effective Sovietisation of urban forms in new Minsk should not be understood in terms of de-nationalization (or Russification), but rather as the successful harmonization of Soviet-style modernization with the Belorussian national narrative. The construction of new Minsk symbolized the transformation of Belorussians from oppressed peasants to modern urbanites and the transition of the former provincial centre into a national capital. Natallia focuses on two particular aspects of this development: the debate over the architectural design of the main artery of the city, Stalin Avenue, in 1944–1948, and on the development of large housing settlements for tractor factory workers in 1946–1960.

In his two contributions, Nari Shelekpayev in a way continues from where Natallia stopped, and focuses on the post-socialist transition and transformation of the Soviet-style national capital into the symbolic centre of the fully independent Kazakh nation. Nari's first piece discusses the relocation of the national capital from Almaty to Astana and shows how, through appropriation of city-space, Kazakh elites attempted to forge the Kazakh nation. Until the collapse of the USSR, Kazakh identity remained rather weak. Nari focuses on the conscious attempt by the authorities to transform the main "ceremonial square" of socialist Kazakhstan, Republic Square in Almaty, into the symbolic central place of the nation in the early 1990s. According to Nari, the attempted transformation, symbolized by the erection of the huge monument celebrating the Nomadic Myth, failed, because it was compromised by pre-existing material structures (Brezhnev era houses) and because it was limited in scope by a lack of free space for more profound alterations in the cityscape. Furthermore, he argues that mobilization of the common past as a basis for the new identity was ineffective. Therefore, the architects of the nation turned to the future. The construction of the new metropolis in Astana, separated from the lived history of not only the former capital in Almaty but also from other parts of Astana itself, should be seen as a major attempt at detachment from the past. Similar to the Stalin Avenue in Minsk, the new national centre in Astana was created as a materialization of the promise of the modernization of the nation and its incorporation into the larger community (in the 1940s Soviet, in the 1990s global).

The second paper on Kazakhstan represents a specific approach towards the materialization of identity in the cityscape. It discusses the form of "banal" nationalization achieved through the politics of re-naming. Nari analyses the strategies of place-naming applied in both post-socialist capitals Almaty and Astana. Urban toponymy, he argues, could not be interpreted in terms of a clear-cut transition, a discontinuity: the designation of toponyms reflected the internal dynamic of the identity building process, which seems to be evolutionary rather than revolutionary. Toponyms associated with the Russian colonial era and Soviet communism have been gradually replaced by names more in accordance with the new national narrative – those of legendary and historical figures from Kazakhstan and Central Asia. Such a vernacularization process is not exclusively concerned with personalities, but sometimes takes the shape of simple translations (Mir – Bejbitshilik). The contested articulation of the new national narrative through urban space manifested itself also in the reflection of foreign policy orientation. The broader self-positioning of the nation in the transnational sphere in post-Soviet Kazakhstan was characterized by conflict between pan-Turkic aspirations and pro-Russian Eurasian affinities. Gradually, reflecting the policy of President Nazarbayev, place-names honouring leading figures of Eurasianism became more frequent, especially in the new capital of Astana. When compared with Almaty, the urban toponymy of the new metropolis became more oriented towards state symbols. Partly, this can be ascribed to the character of the city, built in a way from scratch and thus lacking a particularly strong local memory.

The chapter by Ivana Nikolovska deals with the controversial project *Skopje 2014*, a massive transformation of the historical centre of Skopje, which became the capital of the newly established state of Macedonia, a name that is no less disputed. As the author argues, the project was first and foremost a top-down enterprise by the new state elites and was executed with the declared objective of re-signifying the city as vigorous, Macedonian, and genuinely European. As a consequence, however, several historical layers, and, by extension, significant components of local memory were doomed to eradication, namely the layer of the Ottoman urban heritage that had significantly imprinted itself on the local architectural tradition, and the layer of socialist/Yugoslav urbanism that was – somewhat ironically – partly designed by Kenzo Tange, the internationally renowned Japanese architect, after the disastrous earthquake which hit the city in 1963. Moreover, the construction and reconstruction of dozens of buildings, statues, and façades stirred up the issue of the unequal representation of different ethnic groups in the multi-ethnic state. The core of the study is preoccupied with the public discourse that surrounded the project and traces the arguments of the promoters of the project and especially the highly contradictory reactions of both the professional and the lay public. These ranged from rather positive responses that praised the vigour of the city, the aesthetic uplifting of the city-centre and the self-confident promotion of national identity, to highly critical comments that targeted the excessive economic costs, the low quality and the inappropriateness of the architectural style, the disrespect for the older traditions of local urban and architectural development, and the harmful implications for the identity of the ethnically diverse Macedonian society.

The final chapter, written by Olga Niutenko, focuses on post-socialist identity building in Moldova. In Moldova, memory of the USSR and socialism (as a particular version of post-socialist) became a particularly critical feature of identity building practices. First, Niutenko offers a short historical excursus in which she describes how Soviet identity was inscribed in Moldovan urban spaces. Post-war Moldova witnessed several decades of Soviet-driven prosperity and modernization, which translated into the fundamental transformation of Moldovan cities.

Such transformation unfolded along the lines described in this volume in the case of Minsk. Soviet ideology blended with the construction of the national identity. However, in Moldova harmonization of the Soviet (Russian) and Moldovan (i.e., linguistically and traditionally Romanian) identity was territorially divided. Chisinau enjoyed the status of the official capital of the Soviet Republic of Moldova and the central place of the Moldovan nation. Tiraspol, urban centre of the region of Transnistria, became a locus of economic modernization, marked by massive industrialization and immigration of workers from the USSR. In the 1990s, this translated into the formulation of two mutually opposing national narratives: the Chisinau-based government of the now independent Moldova built its national identity around re-invented Romanian roots, while the Russian-speaking population in Transnistria formulated its national identity based on the remembrance of the Soviet and Russian past. This division, however, did not take the form of an abrupt change. Olga analyses the manifestation of the identity construction process in urban space and concludes that in both cases the re-writing of urban memory (toponymy, monuments) and its mobilization occurred gradually, reflecting the social, political and economic dynamics in the region. Olga observes that representation of the Soviet past is emblematic of the growing differences in materialized identities in Chisinau and Tiraspol urban space since the 1990s.

Society and Space in (Post-)Socialist Cities: Directions in Research

Natallia Linitskaya

Introduction

The socialist city can be approached from several perspectives. Economic geographers, known as the so-called "ecological school," regard it as a specific product of common large-scale processes of modernisation. Socialist urbanism is seen as deficient, in many respects, a delayed variant of development, compared to the capitalist modernity. According to this logic, the post-socialist city is currently in the process of returning to the capitalist path. From the historical perspective, the socialist city is rather understood as a product of the European utopian thinking, a particular construct, which is genetically bound with the (socialist) mode of production and thus linked to a specific political and cultural context and the role of politics. The control over the allocation and distribution of resources and the centralised planning of production and consumption together with priority given to heavy industry resulted in a specific type of urbanity, as the scholars of the so-called "historical school" claim. According to Ivan Szelenyi, who adopted the latter position, the socio-political context made the socialist cities less urbanized in three key aspects, compared to its capitalist counterpart: the socialist cities were less diverse in terms of services; they had fewer (visible) marginalities, ranging from urban creative subcultures to beggars and criminals; and they were less densely built, as the urban planners could be more generous in using the space.[46]

---

46   Sonia Hirt, "Whatever Happened to the (Post)Socialist City?," *Cities* 32, Suppl. 1 (2013), pp. 29–38; Ivan Szelenyi, "Cities under Socialism – and After," *Cities after Socialism. Urban and Regional Change and Conflict in Post-Socialist Societies*, Gregory Andrusz – Michael Harloe – Ivan Szelenyi (eds.), Oxford: Blackwell Publishers 1996, pp. 286–317.

To provide another definition, Thomas Bohn formulated a set of specific features that are characteristic for the socialist city: no respect towards private property, division of the city space in axes marked with high-rise buildings, a monumental representative centre with administrative buildings and ceremonial squares, lots of public space including parks with socialist monuments, monotonous housing estates, a system of distribution engendering social segregation, as well as mistakes in suburbanisation.[47] From a historical point of view, the utopian, imaginary dimension of the socialist city comes to the fore as a fully-fledged factor that not only affected the space-formation by influencing the mind-set of architects and politicians, but that also created the foundation of everyday life and hence of legitimacy of the regime in the eyes and heads of the citizens. The city served the Bolsheviks as a tool of forging "correct consciousness," an integral image affecting the senses and imagination. Ideology moulded places, modes of behaviour, and even the emotional reactions of people who, on their part, fashioned the reality of city.[48]

This chapter aims to offer a perspective on research into the socialist and post-socialist city on the grounds of the papers presented at the biennial conferences organised by the European Association for Urban History (EAUH) in 2006–2014. Particular attention is devoted to papers which deal with post-war East-European cities. Three themes were of particular importance for the conferences' presenters: interpretations of the social roles of architecture; examination of the behaviour it shaped; and research into the paths of transformations of the spatial memory. The overview is therefore divided along these clusters. The first section deals with studies on socialist design understood as political promises of happiness. Papers that are taken into account in the second section touch on the "tactics" of the population in response to the official discourses on societal norms. The final section provides a glimpse at papers that focused on the memory and transformation of urban spaces in the post-socialist

47 Thomas Bohn, "Zur Einleitung," *Von der "europäischen Stadt" zur "sozialistischen Stadt" und zurück? Urbane Transformationen im östlichen Europa des 20. Jahrhunderts*, Thomas Bohn (ed.), München: Oldenburg Verlag 2009, pp. 1–20, here p. 9.

48 Maya Grekova, "The City as Space of Difference: Roma in Socialist Sofia," paper presented at the 8th Conference of the European Association for Urban History (Stockholm 2006), Session M15 The Socialist City – Concepts and Realities between Utopianism and Pragmaticism (Eliza Stanoeva – Nicole Münnich – Tanja Damljanović – Vladimir Kulić, orgs.). Further in the text, the conferences are refered to as "EAUH conference;" the EAUH conferences have been held biennially since 1992; for information about the Association, the list of all biennial conferences, and the database of papers, see the Association website. Accessible at: www .eauh.eu.

period. What constitutes a common thread, observable in the papers, is the shift of focus from the uniqueness of the Soviet Avant-Garde to the broader social significance of Socialist Realism, which was hitherto obscured in the public mind through the ideological framework of the Cold War. The question of the "relevance of Socialist Realism as to its symbolic and economic value" was thus opened up in the discussions.[49] In addition, the place of Socialist Realism in architecture was revisited with regard to local cultural traditions of the countries of the Eastern bloc, and its relation to modernism was reinterpreted, pointing to the their shared ideological underpinnings rather than contradictions.[50]

The chapter is opened by a brief glance over Henri Lefebvre's and Michel de Certeau's theoretical notions related to the endeavours in Sovietology regarding the role of ideology in everyday life and the formation of subjectivities. Without providing an overview of recent studies in Sovietology, which is beyond the scope of this chapter, we should argue that it is instructive to study socialist society using the optics of a socialist city. Social change is rooted in the Enlightenment period and the welfare state discourse as a study on the city of Magnitogorsk pointed out.[51] As short as it is, the extract from Lefebvre's understanding of space provides the reader with the importance of space-construction in the socialist state, be it exercised in a constructivist or socialist realist manner.

Life-Building Space

Thinking about space in relation to social questions has preoccupied social scientists at least since the Renaissance, when Thomas More wrote his famous "Utopia." Perfectly organised space was seen as the necessary

---

49 Kimberly Zarecor, "Landscape of Socialist Realist Imagination. Reality and Unreality in the Construction of New Ostrava, Czechoslovakia," paper presented at the 8th EAUH Conference (Stockholm 2006), Session M15, The Socialist City – Concepts and Realities between Utopianism and Pragmaticism (Eliza Stanoeva – Nicole Münnich – Tanja Damljanović – Vladimir Kulić, orgs.), p. 9.

50 Anders Åman pointed at the fact that aesthetic judgment can become entrapped in ideological discourse, either socialist or modernist. See his *Architecture and Ideology in Eastern Europe during the Stalin Era*, New York: The MIT Press 1992. Kimberly Elman Zarecor has recently suggested that the centralised system of governing under communism was well-compatible with the modernist rationalisation of architecture which resulted in panel construction in the East and West. See her *Manufacturing Socialist Modernity: Housing in Czechoslovakia, 1945–1960*, Pittsburgh: University of Pittsburgh Press 2011.

51 Stephen Kotkin, *Magnetic Mountain. Stalinism as Civilization*, Los Angeles – Berkeley: California University Press 1997, p. 19.

condition for the perfection of society. For this reason, it is not surprising that the understanding of space and society as isomorphic came to mind among the leftist circles. Henri Lefebvre, a French Marxist, suggested that space was an active social force: the layout of space is organised by the social order, which, in turn, is simultaneously reproduced by space.[52] The so-called "social space" was further analyzed as consisting of the conceived, perceived, and occupied space. The social spatiality of city then arises from the relations between these three spaces, which manifest themselves both in form of representations and practices.[53]

Lefebvre sees the city as the combination of production and a product: urbanism, being dependent on the mode of production, reproduces the relations of production. Hence, the unique and the repetitive, the artistic practices as well as the mechanical processes cannot be separated in their "common movement" from the production of space.[54] This kind of understanding is further uncovered in the concept of "secondary creativity" introduced by Michel de Certeau. De Certeau speaks of consumers, who become creative by dint of simply using space for purposes different from those planned by those in power. Arranged into a geometrical order and named by the power, a place is actualised into an anthropological space by means of everyday practice of it. To use a place means to give a direction as well as temporality to it, with various levels of accessibility existing, and in such way "spatial stories" obtain their shape.[55] Every life story not only takes place in it, but creates its own space and is affected by it. De Certeau draws out an analogy with speech acts to develop his approach to space. Just as the appropriation of language happens through speech acts, space is mastered by the process of walking through the city.[56]

De Certeau's attention to the practices of the "silent mass of consumers" in a capitalist society is linked to the distinction of socialist society as an active social agent. The ideological representation of space, which is understood by de Certeau as "strategy," is appropriated "tactically" in daily lives via an "ensemble of movements" on the part of individuals. Let us bear in mind that the pragmatics behind choices was stipulated within a system of values formed with the active participation of ideolo-

---

52 Henri Lefebvre, *The Production of Space*, English trans. Donald Nicholson-Smith, Oxford: Blackwell Publishers 1991.
53 Ibid., p. 288.
54 Ibid.
55 Michel de Certeau, *The Practice of Everyday Life*, English trans. by Stephen Randall, Berkeley: University of California Press 1984, p. 117.
56 Ibid., p. xiii.

Figure 2.1 Kazan', Dom Pechati. [The House of Print]. This building dates back to 1935, and was constructed by Semion Pehn. Late 1920s and first half of 1930s was time, in which Constructivism became acknowledged not only as avant-garde, but as common style for civil constructions. This very period was formative for soviet urban culture and soviet spaces, be they routine or representative, were rendered in this style. (Photo by Rafail Abramovich Mazelev, Kombinat izoprodukcii №1, Leningrad, 1965. A postcard from the collection of S. A. Prokopovich).

gy. Society actively used spaces delimited by power representatives and articulated within the language of ideology. Political will defined everyday life – what was normal and what was deviant, what was beautiful and what was ugly – by fixing meanings to certain spaces.[57] The socialist space is thus understood in relation to the presence of ideology that provokes a specific type of action. How did ideas arrange physical space and how did people live such spaces?

In the eyes of modernist urban planners, including those of socialist orientation, space is conceived in its universality, represented by a plan, and underlined with the idea of a rational disposition of space that reflects specific social functions. Those who defined space had political power. In this respect, Soviet Constructivists, to whom space was ab-

---

57 Introduction to Session M49 Everyday Life in the Socialist City (Jana Nosková – Slavomíra Ferenčuhová – Barbora Vacková – Lucie Galčanová, orgs.) held at the 11th EAUH Conference (Prague 2012).

stract, merely a container for architectural objects, and Soviet state planning institutions shared the way of conceiving space. Functional zones
based on the demands of production sites, divided space as to where
to work, live, and play, as well as time for these activities. The ratio-
nalist drive of urban planners made them think of separating all human needs – such as eating, communicating, raising children – into the
public sphere, and reduce private life merely to the time for sleeping in
private cells of otherwise collective houses. For example, one of the projects for Magnitogorsk envisioned organising the city into specific belts:
separated from the production belt with the belt for transportation and
greenery, a belt for housing followed, with towers set amidst greenery.[58]
We can conclude that the urban plan dictated the way of life: it could
promote either the solitude of car owners, living in individual houses
along the road, or a collective existence in communal flats, as reflected in
the debate between "urbanists" and "de-urbanists disurbanists."[59] In this
context, it should be pointed out that modernist projects in the Soviet
Union and in the West had much in common. As we shall see, people
successfully adjusted the plans and sometimes even themselves.

Constructivism and Socialist Realism Revisited

Historian of architecture Kimberly Zarecor has suggested there were
three traits characteristic for socialist design: equality, utilitarian form,
and technical innovativeness.[60] The socialist style is thus put within the

58 The project of Ivan Leonidov for Magnitogorsk, 1930. Nikolaj Petrovich Bylinkin – Aleksandr
Vasilevich Rjabushin, *Istorija sovetskoj arkhitektury* [History of Soviet Architecture], Moskva:
Stojizdat 1985, p. 23.
59 In 1929–1930, a debate between two groupings of modernist-minded architects, economists
and other social scholars were formed in USSR around the question of a form of socialist settlement. It was believed that the urban question (that is, lack and insufficiency of housing, bad
sanitary conditions) would be resolved under socialism. One grouping, "urbanists", argued
for urbanisation by condensing people in the tower-like collective houses, where people will
live in a collective way. Another party – "disurbanists" – proposed the dissolution of cities and
the development of automobile roads instead, along which light construction would accom-
modate individuals. Either vision was supposed to be deployed on a country-wide scale. The
argument was rapidly put to an end by the Stalinist state for the reason of the "utopian character" of these plans. See Ivan Nevzgodin, "The Socialist City behind the Scenes: the Crucial
Theoretical Debate in Moscow," paper presented at the 8th EAUH Conference (Stockholm
2006), Session M15 The Socialist City – Concepts and Realities between Utopianism and Pragmaticism (Eliza Stanoeva – Nicole Münnich – Tanja Damljanović – Vladimir Kulić, orgs.).
60 Kimberly Zarecor, "Landscape of the Socialist Imagination: Reality and Unreality in the Construction of New Ostrava, Czechoslovakia," paper presented at the 8th EAUH Conference

context of "international," along the intellectual line leading from the rationalism of the Enlightenment and culminating in the modernism of Le Corbusier as formulated in the Athens Charter (1933). The problematics of Socialist Realism, Classicist variation, as the successor of Avant-Garde still intrigues scholars and is connected to the nature of Stalinism, defined as modernisation with traditional traits.[61] Socialist Realism was dismissed as a blind alley of style by modernist architects who flirted with the idea of revolution as the answer for urban questions, charmed with the audacity of the early Soviet designs, and in agreement with the socialist reformist vocation of architecture.[62] Recently, an understanding of the Avant-Garde was refined due to the understanding of architecture in a broad social context.

The principles of Socialist Realism were set forth in 1934 at the First Assembly of the Union of Soviet Writers and reformulated by the Union of Architects in 1937. These principles required that a building was to create an artistic image, be both ideological (ideinyj) and truthful (pravdivyj), meet the technological, cultural and social demands of housing, and be cost-effective and perfectly executed. The socialist realist building was to be aesthetically beautiful, comfortable to live in, and express the joy and aspirations of its inhabitants at that time.[63] In the formula of architecture, in which technology and art work together to fulfill the social function, priority was given to art, to the image. The image of richness, stability and harmony was found in the examples of the Antiquity period, Italian Renaissance and Russian Classicism. Buildings were to be connected to one another by axial perspectives, based on symmetry with a few ideal points of perspective.[64] Such a city was above all an idea; it was finished on paper immediately, but it often remained incomplete in reality.

(Stockholm 2006), Session M 15 The Socialist City – Concepts and Realities between Utopianism and Pragmaticism (Eliza Stanoeva – Nicole Münnich – Tanja Damljanović – Vladimir Kulić, orgs.), p. 2.

61 Moshe Lewin, *The Soviet Century*, London: Verso 2005; Boris Groys, *Gesamtkunstwerk Stalin*, Moskva: Ad Marginem 2013.

62 See for example, Anatol Kopp, *Ville et révolution. Architecture et urbanisme soviétiques des années vingt*, Paris: Anthropos 1969.

63 Architect and scholar Vjacheslav Glazychev points out that neglect of economical and technological sides distorted the essence of architecture as an art form essentially connected to social life. Vjacheslav Leonidovich Glazychev, *Teoreticheskie osnovy sovetskoj arkhitektury* [Theoretical Foundations of Soviet Architecture], Moskva: Strojizdat 1984, p. 206, 207.

64 Andrej Vladimirovich Ikonnikov – Georgij Petrovich Stepanov, *Ehstetika socialisticheskogo goroda* [Aesthetics of the Socialist City], Moskva: Izdatelstvo Akademii Khudozhestv 1963, p. 204.

Figure 2.2 Cheboksary, Chuvash State music-drama theatre named after K. V. Ivanov. This building is an example of the postwar Socialist Realism: retrospective, based on symbolism and enjoying rich architectural décor. Antique patterns were to express the greatness of the socialist culture. (Photo by Il'ja Abramovich Narovlianskij, Kombinat izoprodukcii №1, Leningrad, 1964. A postcard fom the collection of S. A. Prokopovich).

Since the second half of the 1930s, Constructivism was driven away from the Soviet building practice. Without denying the coercive power of the Stalinist state, I adopt the view, along with some Russian scholars, that the state rather followed the already existing demand of Soviet society, both of the cultural elite and ordinary citizens who came to the city from villages and expected to see beauty in the traditional sense.[65] At the same time, architectural trends had also developed independently from the state order, however without the possibility to disregard its kitsch or gigantic and megalomanic images. One can think about the genuine re-opening of the Classics on the part of Soviet architects who reinterpreted the old masters because they provided them with the necessary

---

65   See Andrej Vladimirovich Ikonnikov, *Prostranstvo i forma v arkhitekture i gradostroitelstve* [Space and Form in Architecture and Urban Planning], Moskva: KomKniga 2006, pp. 312–313. A useful volume presenting different views on the topic is *Arkhitektura stalinskoj ehpokhi: Opyt istoricheskogo osmyslenija* [Architecture of the Stalin Time. Experience of Historical Insight], Julija Leonidovna Kosenkova (ed.), Moskva: KomKniga 2010.

instruments for an expression corresponding with the social situation. Thus, the socialist reconstruction of Moscow, begun by 1935, provided an iconic image of the socialist city. Together with the general "blagous-trojstvo" (improvement) – the alignment and widening of streets, install-ing facilities – the exemplary Gorky street in Moscow came into being together with voluminous buildings that impressed contemporaries, in the same way as the Moscow metro did. Socialist Realism, which had borrowed functional solutions worked out by the Avant-Gardists aiming to change the life of the people, turned even more revolutionary as to its effects on social consciousness.[66]

Let us now look at the realisations of design. Making use of the term "spatial stories," Irina Seits presented the Narva Gate district in Len-ingrad as a conceptual model of space of early 1920s Constructivism, wherein attention was devoted to the novelty of everyday routine and a new type of people who were to develop in the new public spaces.[67] Seits examines the forms of dwelling, furniture, and fashion, and seeks answers as to why new forms did not materialise in practice. She con-cludes that collectivism was promoted from above but that it was not popular among the people.[68] The failure of the supply system and of efficient building processes generated a negative response on the part of the population who were annoyed with the absence of kitchens.[69] It seems that the Avant-Gardist projects were not viable. Yet, the political initiative of the Avant-Garde should be also taken into account as it led to the repression of the previously mentioned.

The implementation of socialist schemes during post-war Stalinisa-tion was far from being identical everywhere in the socialist camp. Hu-bert Guzik traces the way through which the idea of collective living was realised after the Second World War, referring to the industrial towns of Zlín and Litvínov as examples. The author formulates his question in the title of his paper "How Collective Were Czechoslovak Collective Houses?" He then probes mental dispositions, cultural experiences and social conditions to find the answer. The gap between the idea and real-

66 Andrej Vladimirovich Ikonnikov, *Arkhitektura XX veka. Utopii i realnost* [Architecture of the XXth Century: Utopias and Reality], Moskva: Progress-Tradicija 2001, p. 286.
67 Irina Seits, "Urban Memory Place of 1920s in St. Petersburg: Reconstruction of Everyday Life in New Socialist District of Narva Gates and its Reenactments in the Present," paper presented at the 11th EAUH Conference (Prague 2012), Session M49 Everyday Life in the Socialist City (Jana Nosková – Slavomíra Ferenčuhová – Barbora Vacková – Lucie Galčanová, orgs.), p. 3.
68 Ibid., p. 4.
69 Stephen Kotkin, *Magnetic Mountain. Stalinism as Civilization*, Los Angeles – Berkeley: Califor-nia University Press 1997, p. 122.

ity serves as a productive ground for research supported by sociological surveys conducted at that time. Guzik infers that the Stalinist notion of collectivism did not take root among Czechoslovak workers since they had their own understanding of what a proper dwelling should look like. In this case, again, the preferences and expectations of society turned out to overweigh immediate political trends. Hence, collective houses were rather rare, and if they happened to be realised, then in a more family-like style, on a more intimate scale.[70]

The idea of socialist urbanism was incarnated in its most pure form in the design of towns that were built on green fields and that bordered industrial complexes, such as steel-work "giants." The principles organising them, the number of inhabitants, and the transportation network were defined by the needs of industrial production. Space of an exemplary socialist city was conceived as "conquered" (in the words of Lefebvre) and rationed out by the state, which monopolised its production.

Socialist Realism moulded the architectural face according to the formula "socialist in content, national in form," following the aim to root communist constructionism in the historical tradition of the respective country. In the GDR, it was Classicism that was seen as expression of the German spirit of rationality and order of the Enlightenment, whilst in Czechoslovakia and Poland, the Renaissance was chosen as the style that corresponded with the "golden ages" in both national narratives.[71] City names, be it Nová Ostrava, Nowa Huta, Sztalinváros, or Stalinstadt, highlighted the supremacy of novelty, the power of political authority, and the mightiness of industry that was responsible for their very existence. The subsequent change of these names, from Sztalinváros to Dunaújváros, from Stalinstadt to Eisenhüttenstadt, only articulated the change of the political (dis)course.

Béla Kerekgyártó introduces the term "paradigmatic city," which he elucidates through the socialist past and contemporary reality of Dunaújváros that emerged and was fashioned as a result of deliberate political decisions. The meshing of the latter with the modernist tradition led to incoherent results, wherein modernist and socialist realist visions

70 Hubert Guzik, "How Collective Were Czechoslovak Collective Houses?," paper presented at the 11th EAUH Conference (Prague 2012), Session S24 New Towns East, West and In-between (Ana Kladnik – Muriel Blaive, orgs.).

71 Michaela Marek, "Die Idealstadt im Realsozialismus. Versuchen zu den Traditionen ihrer Notwendigkeit," *Sozialgeschichtliche Kommunismusforschung: Tschechoslowakei, Polen, Ungarn und DDR. 1948–1968*, Christianne Brenner – Peter Heumos (eds.), München: Oldenbourg 2005, pp. 425–480, here p. 432.

often clashed, the author concludes, and hence, the centre was never finished.[72]

When functionality was back in the 1950s, "form" was no more articulated among the objectives of architecture; on the contrary, "image" remained in first place. Although Soviet architects had a profound training in Constructivism, the effect was degraded by the command-administrative system. Maximal simplicity of façades was required and open floor plans were seen as a means for achieving freedom. The houses thus degenerated into bedroom communities from where architectural detail was excluded as an economic burden for house-constructing factories. Monotonous forms, often without sufficient infrastructure, became an expression of the lack of possibilities under communism.[73]

In his paper, Henning Schulze refers to the socialist urban concept as "hypertrophic."[74] He analyses this concept through the example of Halle-Neustadt, a town for workers of the chemical combines Leuna and Buna. The ideas put in service of this new urbanism and making of the new Man were "optimism, education, work ethic, and egalitarianism in housing."[75] Ambivalence in socialist housing policy appears in the memories of the inhabitants. On the one hand, the flats were comfortable, though the monotonous design was exhaustive.[76] On the other hand, the plants and their work shifts defined the time for everything: transportation, dining, and class hours for kindergartens and schools. The expectations of a happy tomorrow with "hot water in each bathtub" showed its dark underside in the melancholy of routine.[77] The aesthetic expression of late socialism consisted of the rationalisation and industrialisation of living.

72 Béla Keregyártó, "The Present of the Recent Past: the Difficult Transformation of a 'Paradigmatic Socialist City.' The Case of Dunaújváros (Former Stalin City)," paper presented at the 9th EAUH Conference (Lyon 2008), Session S19, The Post-Socialist City: Continuity and Change in Urban Space and Imagery (Alfrun Kliems – Marina Dmitrieva, orgs.), pp. 22–23.

73 For a perspective on Eastern and Western housing estates see Javier Monclús Fraga – Carmen Díez Medina, "Modernist Housing Projects in Western and Eastern Socialist European Cities: How Different?," paper presented at the 12th EAUH Conference (Lisbon 2014), Session M37 Iron Curtain Cities? Urban Space in Cold War Europe (Moritz Fölmer – Marc B. Smith, orgs.).

74 Henning Schulze, "Routines and Disturbances in the Cognitive Economy of Socialist Cities in GDR – the Example Halle-Neustadt," paper presented at the 11th EAUH Conference (Prague 2012), Session M49 Everyday Life in the Socialist City (Jana Nosková – Slavomíra Ferenčuhová – Barbora Vacková – Lucie Galčanová, orgs.), p. 3.

75 Ibid., pp. 3–4.

76 Ibid., p. 4.

77 Ibid.

A story of building enthusiasm is embodied in the construction of the housing complex MDM in Warsaw, which began in 1950. Martina Obarska renders an image of the district through the analysis of layers of the ideological discourse and subjective experience.[78] Through the exploration of imagination and memory, it appears that the MDM was an amalgam of "sacred" and everyday space. On an everyday level, the space fell apart into spatial cases of inequality, where restaurants and rooms were open for some to wine and dine, while the construction site and piles of ruins in the backyard were set aside for the drinking and dwelling of others.[79]

Ana Kladnik shows the interplay between representations of the new urban space and its perceptions. She explains how the legitimisation of the superiority of socialism rested in the availability of modern amenities for workers. Particularly in Velenje, a Yugoslav city, the effect was achieved in the quality of flats and in their modern design.[80] The system of state planning and distribution defined where one could live so that one could live well. Facilitated space aimed at supporting the regime and at stabilising society. People perceived a range of amenities and an agreeable district as a set of conditions for a happy life. Kladnik finds a thread connecting state priorities to people's desires and needs. As for how happy living was actually proceeding in the mining towns of Velenje and Havířov, the author looks at the rules of distribution, the ways of obtaining housing, mechanisms of investment, and systems of credit in order to gauge the level of approval and enthusiasm on the part of the population.[81]

Spaces and images of a joyful life become inseparable as they are formed in interaction, in a common movement, in the words of Lefebvre. Kimberly Zarecor also proposes that Socialist Realism provided material for the imagination of communism as a common well-being, in contrast to the prior state of misery of workers' housing. Blocs of "cheap and aesthetically pleasing housing" were meant to be perceived as expressions of

---

78 Martina Obarska, "Spatial Stories: Socialist Realistic District through the Eyes of its Residents," paper presented at the 11th EAUH Conference (Prague 2012), Session M49 Everyday Life in the Socialist City (Jana Nosková – Slavomíra Ferenčuhová – Barbora Vacková – Lucie Galčanová, orgs.), p. 2.

79 Ibid., p. 5.

80 Ana Kladnik, "Socialist Towns – Symbols of the New Society: Building a Socialist Town in Yugoslavia and Czechoslovakia," paper presented at the 9th EAUH Conference (Lyon 2008), Session M22 Authoritarian Urbanism – Politics and Design in European Communist and Fascist Cities since 1917 (Kimberly Elman Zarecor – Feruccio Trabalzi, orgs.), p. 31.

81 Ibid., p. 39.

Figure 2.3 Poruba-Nová Ostrava, Kandlův dům z průčelí. [The House of Kandl, front façade view]. Building and reconstructing cities in socialist realist manner was used as a means of Sovietisation of Eastern Europe. An ambitious project of New Ostrava, reduced in the end to a district, appealed with the comfort of housing that was claimed to be available to workers only under Socialism. (Orbis, Prague, from the beginning of the 1960s. A postcard from the collection of S. A. Prokopovich).

state care. Zarecor's object of concern is housing policy in Nová Ostrava, where she shows socialism as a project of modernity physically embodied in socialist realist housing. This project takes on diverse aesthetic forms, combining the technique of typification with the Greek order of adorning panel housing together with decorative elements borrowed from the architecture of the Renaissance.[82]

In fact, Socialist Realism could take diverse forms in order to please local tastes. Erika Szívós revisits the socialist districts of Budapest from the 1950s and 1960s. She puts these projects within the modernist traditi-

82 Kimberly Zarecor, "Landscape of the Socialist Imagination: Reality and Unreality in the Construction of New Ostrava, Czechoslovakia," paper presented at the 8th EAUH Conference (Stockholm 2006), Session M15 The Socialist City – Concepts and Realities between Utopianism and Pragmaticism (Eliza Stanoeva – Nicole Münnich – Tanja Damljanović – Vladimir Kulić, orgs.), p. 2.

on to build nicely and to elaborate floor-plans.[83] Szívós discerns whether or not communist housing was that bad by checking the polls of public opinion that were undertaken in order to obtain feedback from the population. The answer turns out to point in the direction of a liveable neighbourhood: despite being planned from above, the construction of new districts succeeded in creating a connection between the space and the people.[84] Marcus Keller compared experimental housing in Budapest with Hansaviertel in West Berlin. Both designs were projected with the same aim, to represent and confirm the legitimacy and capability of the respective political powers. The Hungarian failure to provide a general plan can be explained by the weakness of public discourse on architecture under communism,[85] while in the West, this very discourse, mastered by specialists, prescribed to people the norms of comfort and beauty.

Shaping Criminal, Contesting for Happiness

The idea of social equality as part of a broader discourse on human happiness inherently bore repressive rationality by excluding the possibility of otherness. Within the totalising ideological picture of reality in socialism, a possibility of a non-Soviet way of thinking was always implied, and the limits of correct thinking and behaving were constantly reinterpreted. Piotr Perkowski traces out the way in which space served to construct the idea of normal and deviant in society. He analyses the spatial stories of a place where alcohol is illegally produced and consumed, a den. The official narrative sets the moral boundary between what is allowed and what is transgressive: "a hole in a fence," "a well-trodden path," "an entrance hidden from the eyes." The physical dirt of the place accompanies moral decline. Precisely in contrast with the den, the space outside appears as decent, indeed respectable.[86] Eszter György likewise

---

83 Erika Szívós, "Utopian Nightmare or Livable Neighborhood?," paper presented at the 9th EAUH Conference (Lyon 2008), Session M22 Authoritarian Urbanism – Politics and Design in European Communist and Fascist Cities since 1917 (Kimberly Elman Zarecor – Feruccio Trabalzi, orgs.), p. 66.

84 Ibid., p. 71.

85 Marcus Keller, "Goals and Reactions: the Story of Hansaviertel, Berlin and Experimental Housing Estate of Óbuda," paper presented at the 12th EAUH Conference (Lisbon 2014), Session M37 Iron Curtain Cities? Urban Space in Cold War Europe (Moritz Fölmer – Marc B. Smith, orgs.), p. 12.

86 Piotr Perkowski, "Socialist City and its 'Melina' in the Polish People's Republic," paper presented at the 10th EAUH Conference (Ghent 2010), Session M19 Geographies of Transgres-

proceeds with a discursive approach in her work, which shows the institutional level of imagining marginality. The author focuses, in particular, on social discrimination of Gypsies in socialist society, fitting the cultural narrative of a "dangerous place" into the historical background of marginalisation.[87]

Socialist urbanisation produced a disproportionate centrality of the city in relation to the region, but failed to fashion an urban style within new cities.[88] As for urban life in the case of Sztálinvarós, Sándor Horváth talks about defining urbanity from the angle of state power. He shows how helpless the officials were in making cultured urbanites out of the first-generation of villagers. As an illustration, one could mention the war against drying laundry on balconies, which the housing authorities led with people. Yet what the author demonstrates, when approaching urban reality through the lenses of the official discourse as well as everyday experiences, are the limits of control over the population; or we should rather speak of the limits that were put to the state by the practice of yesterday's villagers who adhered to the routines they had been used to before they moved to the first socialist city. More importantly perhaps, the paper highlights the fact that identities were acquired by people as they were pronounced by the state and within particular conditions. It also reflects, quite interestingly, on the idea of urbanity under socialism as synonymous to civilised behaviour. The process of delimiting and compromising the definition of urban was the essence of socialist transformation, while, in fact, socialist urbanism was a mixture of rural and "civilised" norms.[89]

Urbanisation served the aims of industrialisation, which in turn dampened the former's potential in some respects.[90] Indeed, housing

sion in the History of City (Herbert Reinke – Margo de Koster, orgs.).

87 Eszter György, "'Gypsy Ghetto' in Budapest – Socialist Urban Texts of the 8th District," paper presented at the 10th EAUH Conference (Ghent 2010), Session M19 Geographies of Transgression in the History of City (Herbert Reinke – Margo de Koster, orgs.).

88 Béla Keregyártó, "The Present of the Recent Past: the Difficult Transformation of a 'Paradigmatic Socialist City'. The Case of Dunaújváros (Former Stalin City)," paper presented at the 9th EAUH Conference (Lyon 2008), Session S19, The Post-Socialist City: Continuity and Change in Urban Space and Imagery (Alfrun Kliems – Marina Dmitrieva, orgs.), p. 21.

89 Sándor Horvath, "The Urban Villagers of the First Hungarian Socialist City," paper presented at the 8th EAUH Conference (Stockholm 2006), Session M15 The Socialist City – Concepts and Realities between Utopianism and Pragmaticism (Eliza Stanoeva – Nicole Münnich – Tanja Damljanović – Vladimir Kulić, orgs.), p. 7.

90 György Enyedi, "Urbanization under Socialism," in: *Cities After Socialism. Urban and Regional Change and Conflict in Post-Socialist Societies*, Gregory Andrusz – Michael Harloe – Ivan Szelenyi (eds.), Oxford: Blackwell Publishers 1996, pp. 100–118.

Figure 2.4 Pravda Avenue in Kladno. The angle shows the high-rise buildings in contrast with the workers' houses, thus juxtaposing the modern and the old for the aims of socialist propaganda. Perspective of the avenue symbolizes movement towards the happy socialist future. (Artia-Orbis, Prague, beginning of the 1960s approximately. A postcard from the collection of S. A. Prokopovich).

was of secondary importance for the state and enjoyed financing only indirectly through the funding of enterprises. One of the most powerful tools for forming identities was the state-led distribution of housing that worked on the basis of thousands of regulations and was based on social stratification. In that way, social capital was ascribed from above. This made one's biography a political statement. A distinctly perceptible correlation was established between one's reliability and one's right to housing, and consequently space was visually arranged so as to be the expression of a loyal identity. In order to obtain space, a person ought to be productive at work and, at the same time, in family life, or seem to be such, as Henning Schulze remarks.[91] One had to have a permanent and qualified position in the appropriate enterprise in order to become

---

91 Henning Schulze, "Routines and Disturbances in the Cognitive Economy of Socialist Cities in GDR – the Example Halle-Neustadt," paper presented at the 11th EAUH Conference (Prague 2012), Session M49 Everyday Life in the Socialist City (Jana Nosková – Slavomíra Ferenčuhová – Barbora Vacková – Lucie Galčanová, orgs.), p. 3.

a part of the collective in the house of Litvínov.[92] To have a family, one needed savings in a bank in order to obtain credit to buy a house in Havířov.[93]

In his paper, Dariusz Jarosz concentrates on housing in Poland from the 1950s to the 1980s. Despite reports of success in some areas, there was a shortage of housing in socialist Poland. Many people circumvented queues in order to avoid waiting in them for years before they finally got hold of a place to live in. Indeed, a vicious circle was formed, in which the shortage provoked a transgression of the law, and transgression of the law engendered shortage. The author views housing as a factor of social behaviour and poses the following question: what does one have to do to get a flat in the period under scrutiny? Jarosz finds a causal relation between discontent due to shortages and the collapse of the regime,[94] but the author of the presented review finds that this pathology rather helped to reproduce the system. The Yugoslav experience, for example, proves that transgressions enforced stability. Liljana Blagojević and Alexandar Kušić explore unofficial construction in the period of late socialism in Belgrade. With an example of a bunch of illegal neighbourhoods, some of them poorer, some of a middle-class position, they reveal the movable boundaries of self-governing, the possibilities of negotiation with the state, and initiatives on the part of the people.[95] Since the state tolerated spontaneous civic undertakings, and even included some of these projects into official plans, the authors conclude that the state let the population strive and gain their happiness themselves.[96]

An inquiry into everyday spatial tactics would be incomplete without looking at the alternative music scene. The punk and hippie movements are inextricably joined to the contest over urban space. Ways of altering official urbanism consisted of such behavioural patterns as creating "niches" and "shelters" in flats and clubs of friends. This shelter was

92 Hubert Guzik, "How Collective Were Czechoslovak Collective Houses?," paper presented at the 11th EAUH Conference (Prague 2012), Session S24 New Towns East, West and In-between (Ana Kladnik – Muriel Blaive, orgs.), p. 8.

93 Ana Kladnik, "Happy Living in a New Socialist Town. Construction, Design and the Distribution of the Apartments in Yugoslavia and Czechoslovakia," paper presented at the 9th EAUH Conference (Lyon 2008), Session M09 Urban Planning and the Pursuit of Happiness (Renaissance-Present) (Arnold Bartetzky, Marc Schalenberg, orgs.), pp. 31, 40.

94 Dariusz Jarosz, "Housing Demand in the Polish Peoples' Republic," paper presented at the 11th EAUH Conference (Prague 2012), Session M49 Everyday Life in the Socialist City (Jana Nosková – Slavomíra Ferenčuhová – Barbora Vacková – Lucie Galčanová, orgs.), p. 7.

95 Ibid., p. 6.

96 Ibid., p. 5.

provided by the Protestant Church, or could be reached outside cities, simply in nature.[97] In old European cities, the socialist system of distribution negatively affected the social status of the centres which became a much less esteemed address, accommodating lower social groups and aging people. After the fall of the Berlin Wall, housing in the centre of Leipzig was overwhelmed by squats.[98]

To sum up this part of the chapter, the reviewed conference papers mostly approached socialist urban spaces from a historical perspective and defined socialist cities as a specific variation of urban modernity. The socialist city is seen as a result of welfare state politics set in a broad European context, in which the state plays an essential role by setting regulations and defining norms.[99] The failure of the state in implementing its promise of happiness within the ideal city of well-being and equality stimulated marginal modes of behaviour rather than a conscious protest.[100] Thus, the socialist city is seen as a protean result of the interaction between strategies of power and people's responses. Everyday urban life under socialism is explored in spaces which set the poles of what is allowed and what is deviant.

Memory of Architecture

Space is permeated by memory, be it individual images of childhood or collective memories. The combination of these accounts for anthropologically occupied spaces, which consist of relations and possess identity and history.[101] Space as a subjective experience unfolding the creative reworking of images in cultural contexts is the main motive in the

---

97 Michael Rauhut, "The Conquest of Urban Space Popular Music, Youth Cultures and Everyday Life in the GDR," paper presented at the 11th EAUH Conference (Prague 2012), Session M49 Everyday Life in the Socialist City (Jana Nosková – Slavomíra Ferenčuhová – Barbora Vacková – Lucie Galčanová, orgs.), p. 2.

98 Christian Rau, "Socialist Living in Old 'Capitalist' Cities: Urbanity, Social Inequality and Spatial Experiences in Leipzig (1970–1980)," paper presented at the 12th EAUH Conference (Lisbon 2014), Session M37 Iron Curtain Cities? Urban Space in Cold War Europe (Moritz Fölmer – Marc B. Smith, orgs.).

99 Stephen Kotkin, *Magnetic Mountain. Stalinism as Civilization*, Los Angeles – Berkeley: California University Press 1997, p. 19.

100 Katherine Lebow, "Public Works, Private Lives: Youth Brigades in Nowa Huta in the 1950," *Contemporary European History* 10, no. 2 (July 2001), pp. 199–219.

101 Marc Augé, *Non-places. Anthropology of Super-Modernity*, English trans. by John Howe, London – New York: Verso 2006, p. 52.

work of Walter Benjamin.[102] In addition, the French philosopher Gaston Bachelard revealed in his phenomenological exploration how space serves as a powerful source for poetics.[103] Collective representations form places and create mimetic objects: statues of heroes and rulers, or street names. In a monumental space, Lefebvre argues, and more precisely in the process of reading it, we recognise ourselves as members of the society participating in it.[104] Lefebvre proposed an interpretation of active societal memory, which is embodied in monuments, that very neatly fits the socialist space, since the educational potential of architecture was extensively exploited: either in the language of the classical style or in that of modern facilities, buildings and housing spoke of superiority of the socialist regimes. The city affected the senses as a piece of art, in which single buildings encapsulated a world view.

In order to destroy a society, it is necessary to eliminate its monuments; but in order to change a society, one should use those monuments differently. With this idea, Lefebvre grasps the essence of changes in urban fabric.[105] A plan of monumental propaganda (14th April 1918) according to which old monuments were torn down and new ones glorifying the revolution were erected, and the city space, decorated with the slogans of power according to the example of Tommaso Campanella's "The City of the Sun," the walls of which were covered with instructive frescoes for the education of citizens, turned out to be an event in the life of the socialist cities of no lesser importance than the abolition of private property.[106] Historical memory in the cities of Central and Eastern Europe transformed twice in the twentieth century: in 1945 and again in 1989, and to re-think this double shift poses a great challenge. To what degree then has the post-socialist city changed and in what forms does its past survive to this day? Has space exhausted its signifying capacity? What do these changes tell us about the current state of society? Yet, before we cover the historiography of post-socialist trans-

102 Valter Benjamin, *Berlinskoe detstvo na rubezhe vekov*, Russian trans. by Galina Snezhinskaja. Moskva: Ad Marginem 2012. Valter Benjamin, *Moskovskij dnevnik*, Russian trans. by Sergej Romashko, Moskva: Ad Marginem 2012.

103 Gaston Bachelard, *Poetika prostoru*, Czech trans. by Josef Hrdlička, Prague: Malvern 2009. Russian edition: Gaston Bashljar, *Poehtika prostranstva*, Russian trans. Nina Kulish, Moskva: Ad Marginem 2014.

104 Henri Lefebvre, *The Production of Space*, English trans. by Donald Nicholson-Smith, Oxford: Blackwell Publishers 1991, p. 225.

105 Ibid., p. 221.

106 Andrej Vladimirovich Ikonnikov – Georgij Petrovich Stepanov, *Ehstetika socialisticheskogo goroda* [Aesthetics of the Socialist City], Moskva: Strojizdat 1963, pp. 235–236.

formations, let us quickly return to the relation between architecture and ideology in the past.

After the revolution of 1917, space in Russia changed its quality: it became tightened, divided, and recomposed as the flats of the bourgeoisie were remade into communal apartments. In other cases, a declaration was enough: social housing, which was originally built by a pro-fascist architect for workers in Slovakia in 1941, suited the representation of the progress of socialism in 1946.[107] To create a new sense of space, a slight change was sometimes sufficient: to rename a street, to broaden a square, etc.[108] In her article on the public space of Sofia, Ljubinka Stoilova emphasises the complexity of relations between the political regime and architecture. Neo-classicism with ornamentation alluding to national history satisfied both the authoritarian and totalitarian regimes in power.[109]

It is useful to bear in mind Lefebvre's notion that the mechanical way of production generates similar spaces. Recent studies convincingly show that socialist architecture was rooted in international practice; but different social and economic restraints, in particular greater control on the part of the bureaucratic institutions in the Soviet Union, made the same phenomena seem different: Soviet housing estates look duller than their Western counterparts.[110] If we accept the view that architecture of the totalitarian era and of interwar modernism used congruent concepts, then doubt inevitably arises concerning the very existence of totalitarian architecture as a distinct style. Western modernism can serve "panoptical goals" just as well as Soviet Neo-classicism, and vice versa: a house embellished with a Neo-renaissance graffito can contain as many amenities

---

107 Ana Kladnik, "Socialist Towns – Symbols of the New Society: Building a Socialist Town in Yugoslavia and Czechoslovakia," paper presented at the 9th EAUH Conference (Lyon 2008), Session M22 Authoritarian Urbanism – Politics and Design in European Communist and Fascist Cities since 1917 (Kimberly Elman Zarecor – Feruccio Trabalzi, orgs.), p. 28.

108 Ljubinka Stoilova, "Totalitarian versus Authoritarian Urbanism: Politics and the Design of Sofia in the 1930s–1950s," paper presented at the 9th EAUH Conference (Lyon 2008), Session M22 Authoritarian Urbanism – Politics and Design in European Communist and Fascist Cities since 1917 (Kimberly Elman Zarecor – Feruccio Trabalzi, orgs.), p. 62.

109 Ibid., p. 47.

110 Ivan Nevzgodin, "The Socialist City behind the Scenes: the Crucial Theoretical Debate in Moscow," paper presented at the 8th EAUH Conference (Stockholm 2006), Session M15 The Socialist City – Concepts and Realities between Utopianism and Pragmaticism (Eliza Stanoeva – Nicole Münnich – Tanja Damljanović – Vladimir Kulić, orgs.); Javier Monclús Fraga – Carmen Díez Medina, "Modernist Housing Projects in Western and Eastern Socialist European Cities: How Different?," paper presented at the 12th EAUH Conference (Lisbon 2014), Session M37 Iron Curtain Cities? Urban Space in Cold War Europe (Moritz Fölmer – Marc B. Smith, orgs.).

Figure 2.5 "Leningrad. New districts are growing." [Unknown author]. This image depicts a *mikrorayon*, the urban unit that became typical for the socialist cities since the late 1950s. Panel housing was set in greenery in a free composition; along the borders of the units ran bigger streets, which were connected with transportation arteries. Design aimed at security and provision of social amenities. (Oleg Ivanovich Maslakov, Lenizdat, 1969. A postcard from the collection of S. A. Prokopovich).

as a functionalist one. What is essential is which elements are articulated in relation to what ideology.

Tarik Cyril Amar presented what happened to Lviv when its identity transformed from a Western one to a Soviet one under Stalinism and de-Stalinisation, by analysing the imagination of urban space. He emphasised the "strategy" of re-imagining spaces when a new Soviet narrative was superimposed over the past bourgeois content of places and spaces. Luckily for the city, the old representative spaces suited the new requirements well, but the symbolism often had to be changed. For instance, the Opera House, which accommodated bourgeois culture in the past, was thus adapted for commemorating the unification of Western and Eastern Ukraine in 1939.[111] Two cityscapes in fact co-existed in Lviv

111 Tarik Cyril Amar, "Lwów to Lviv. Soviet Urban Planning and Design in the Soviet West under Stalinization and Destalinization, 1939–1966, paper presented at the 9th EAUH Conference (Lyon 2008), Session M22 Authoritarian Urbanism – Politics and Design in European Communist and Fascist Cities since 1917 (Kimberly Elman Zarecor – Feruccio Trabalzi, orgs.), p. 13.

on the same street, where a monument devoted to Lenin stood opposite to a monument devoted to the Polish national poet Adam Mickiewicz.[112] Urban space tolerates lending itself to diverse stories coexisting one next to the other.

The paper of Lukasz Galusek also informs on the ways of cooperation between memory and history. Analysing the case of Polish cities, particularly Wroclaw and Sejny, he draws on the tool of memory called "imposition." The Polish inhabitants of Wroclaw who settled in the city after the end of the Second World War instead of the expelled Germans came to terms with their discontinuous history on the grounds of building a memory that was congruent with the memory of the city itself; memory was thus superimposed onto history. However, in the small town of Sejny, a complicated history of the nationalist conflict of 1920, which took place between the Poles and the Lithuanians, eliminated the sense of community between people of different nationalities who lived next to each other. Galusek reports on the process of recovering memory, which began in Sejny with the help of theatre and singing meetings.[113]

Mariusz Czepczyński then deals with the theoretical aspect of the cultural landscapes of socialism, particularly with interrogating the transformative effect of memory in the urban fabric, the conditions of the recognition, reinterpretation, and disappearance of the past.[114] In addition, Malgorzata Omilanowska suggests that the path leading away from the socialist "bright future" is not straightforward, as the process of re-thinking one iconic socialist landscape, the case of Plac Defilad in Warsaw, illustrates. The changes the place underwent in the past and is undergoing in the present are quite radical; anyway, the mighty Palace of Culture and Sciences was designated a historical monument in 2007. The building, which embodies the Soviet presence in the past, is planned to acquire a democratic look in the present. Omilanowska comments, however, that the multiple unrealised projects to remake the square – e.g., by creating

112 Ibid., p. 9.

113 Lukasz Galusek, "Cities as Places of Common Memory in Poland at the Turn of the XXth Century – Two Cases: Wroclaw and Sejny," paper presented at the 11th EAUH Conference (Prague 2012), Session M40 Towns Are Made of Memory Places – Towns as Memory Places of Urban Life in 19th and 20th centuries (Andrea Pokludová – Catherine Horel – Pavel Kladiwa, orgs.), pp. 6–9.

114 Mariusz Czepczyński, "Representations and Images of 'Recent History' of Post-Socialist Cities. Liminality and Transition of Landscape Icons," paper presented at the 9th EAUH Conference (Lyon 2008), Session S19, The Post-Socialist City: Continuity and Change in Urban Space and Imagery (Alfrun Kliems – Marina Dmitrieva, orgs.). See his Cultural Landscapes of Post-Socialist Cities: Representations of Powers and Needs, Aldershot: Ashgate 2008.

an artificial lake or a tunnel – have little to do with the understanding of democracy as modesty. Rather, the elements of the old ideology remain, even if modified, under the pressure of collective nostalgia.[115]

Strangely enough, the Avant-Garde heritage of Saint Petersburg acquires little attention, as the editors of one recent book put it, also due to the strong roots of the Classicism tradition in the city, but the reluctance of the inhabitants is socially embedded.[116] The Narva Gate district, with its human-scaled housing, though well-preserved and recognised as a cultural heritage, does not arouse pride in its residents, but rather symbolises the failure of a social experiment in their eyes.[117] On an official level, the Russian state does not shift to seeing the pre-Soviet historical experience as constitutive; on the contrary, it experiences nostalgia for Soviet times.[118] However, this nostalgia lacks reflective self-irony, inherent to German *Ostalgia* for instance. In Lithuania, to give another example, the former cells where KGB-interrogations had taken place were turned into an entertainment spot for tourists who can even spend a night there. This strategy of nation-building underrates historical experience. Lviv, then, still carries on the oblivions inherited from the socialist era, such as not being attentive to the history of the Holocaust.[119]

In the discussion on the contemporary state of affairs in former socialist cities, a concept of so-called "banalisation" was proposed in order to conceptualise what was happening to the traces of socialist cities in our contemporary space, when their sacred meanings were squeezed out by new functions of entertainment, consumerism, and business.[120]

115 Malgorzata Omilanowska, "Defilad Square in Warsaw. How Far Can One Run From Ideology?," paper presented at the 9th EAUH Conference (Lyon 2008), Session S19 The Post-Socialist City: Continuity and Change in Urban Space and Imagery (Alfrun Kliems – Marina Dmitrieva, orgs.), p. 135.

116 Boris Mihajlovich Kirikov – Margarita Sergejevna Stieglitz, *Leningrad. Avant-garde. Architecture: A Guide*, St. Peterburg: Kolo 2009, p. 5.

117 Irina Seits, "Urban Memory Place of 1920s in St. Petersburg Reconstruction of Everyday Life in New Socialist District of Narva Gates and its Reenactments in the Present," paper presented at the 11th EAUH Conference (Prague 2012), Session M49 Everyday Life in the Socialist City (Jana Nosková – Slavomíra Ferenčuhová – Barbora Vacková – Lucie Galčanová, orgs.), p. 9.

118 Olga Andreevna Zinovieva, *Simvoly stalinskoj Moskvy*, Moskva: Izdatelskij dom TONCHU 2009.

119 Marian Prokopovych, "Lviv Interactive: The Pros and the Cons of Urban History Online," paper presented at the 10th EAUH Conference (Ghent 2010), Session S29 The Interactive City Map as a Means of Displaying and Interpreting Urban History (Harald Binder, org.), p. 6.

120 Lydia Coudroy de Lille – Miléna Guest, "Towards Banalization? Transforming the Legacies of the Post-socialist City," in: *The Post-Socialist City: Continuity and Change in Urban Space and*

Figure 2.6 A shopping centre, designed by Prague Urban-Planning Institute in Prosek, the district in Prague with some 9000 apartment units (finished by 1972). Social services were to be dispersed in space gradually in the panel housing residential districts: basic ones such as kindergartens were placed in walking distance, while the administrative, cultural and shopping centres were to be equally accessible to a larger amount of inhabitants. Under-financing often hampered such a harmonious disposition. (Prague, around 1972. From the collection of S. A. Prokopovich).

Transformations reflect the process of accommodation of new values and have political relevance. Politics of memory speaks of the history of these cities and reveals neuralgic points in the collective bodies of the nations.

Minsk, the object of my own research interest, is a perfect example that illustrates how symbolical meanings of architectural style are drifting between political regimes. The image of European values is applied to the urban space that used to be exemplary socialist, and nowadays serves to support the authoritarian regime that submits to loyalty to the Soviet legacy. On the other hand, the absence of a public discourse on the memory of communism prevents socialist ensembles from being un-

Imagery, Alfrun Kliems – Marina Dmitrieva (eds.), Berlin: Jovis Verlag 2011. This book is the result of Session S19 that took place in the 9th Conference (Lyon 2008) under the same title, organised by Alfrun Kliems and Marina Dmitrieva.

derstood precisely as a unique method of urban planning. As a result, they are threatened for the sake of immediate profit although they created the identity of Minsk.

A comparison of Warsaw and Minsk, two cities that were destroyed during the Second World War and rebuilt after its end, is revealing as it regards variety in socialist urbanism. National memory remained decisive for the reconstruction of the capital of Poland. The Castle, destroyed during the Warsaw Uprising of Autumn 1944, was rebuilt in its original form, brick by brick. The reason for this was the feeling of connection through the epochs, which created an "imagined community."[121] On the contrary, in Minsk, everything was rebuilt into something new, something different: for the sake of invented traditions, the Catholic Cathedral turned into a sport centre, a Mauritanian style synagogue into a Russian drama theatre, etc. Belarus circumvented its past and used classical examples of other cultures, beginning history from a certain point at zero. The reconstruction that took place in Minsk in the 1960s brought the demolition of the Old Town. The oldest district Nemiga was torn down soon after its 900th anniversary, despite the appearance of the first law on preserving cultural monuments in 1969. It was not recognised as valuable, and nor was the Romanesque Cold Synagogue that was unlucky enough to be located next to the new headquarters of the Belarusian State Institute for Industrial Design. All things "obsolete" were politically unreliable within ideologised aesthetics. Small craft shops hindered civilised service, crooked streets hindered transportation, and poor sanitary conditions were anti-Soviet and petit-bourgeois. Minsk was dubbed as "old and new"; it was new despite being old, and this was exciting for the planners. Moreover, even the archaeological layer disappeared: the banks of Nemiga and the hill of the old castle were destroyed by bulldozers. With no cultural memory to remain, any change was simply acceptable.

Variations can be seen also in the legacy of the socialist urbanism for contemporary urban development. In cities such as Budapest or Ostrava, schools, parks, kindergartens and cosy courtyards still draw population to socialist neighbourhoods due to the comfort and possibility of socialisation, and also attract a flow of tourism due to their authenticity.[122] On

---

121 Vladimir Sedov, *Pamjat sebja. Korolevskij zamok v Varshave* [Memory of Self. The Royal Palace in Warsaw]. Accessible at: http://www.projectclassica.ru/v_o/06_2003/06_2003_o_07a.htm . Last retrieved 15 February 2016.

122 Erika Szívós, "Utopian Nightmare or Livable Neighborhood?," paper presented at the 9th EAUH Conference (Lyon 2008), Session M22 Authoritarian Urbanism – Politics and Design

the other hand, problems of badly designed spaces are retained. With regard to contemporary Dunaújváros, for instance, privatisation did not really improve people's standard of living. Municipalities are in decline, infrastructures do not provide possibilities for work and education, the youth of the city is significantly reduced, and the population is aging.[123]

As the papers made clear, the post-socialist cities provide us with a distinct perspective for observing the changes which the postmodern world brings with it. One speaks of different variants of post-socialist urbanism the same as of socialist schemes that were installed into various historical situations and differed from country to country.[124] Those transformations into which public spaces launch themselves on the basis of re-casted identities and transmuted cultures still call for a thorough explanation. A subtler interpretation of city topography is still a task which requires urban historians to develop a sensitivity to the most common meanings that escape critique, precisely because they remain the unnoticeable, which is there as the very fabric of our own lives. The socialist city is not confined to the imagination as spaces of childhood which sometimes pass as a dim wave in the walls of buildings made from non-transparent glass. It still lingers in contemporary urban spaces.

Conclusion

There was a variety of socialist cities: old European towns, the spaces of which were adjusted to the socialist regimes, as in the case of Leipzig; sites built on green grass next to large industrial enterprises such as Eisenhüttenstadt, Nowa Huta or Magnitogorsk; cities rebuilt after the Second World War like Minsk, or those that appropriated a distinct look as the result of reconstruction activities such as Moscow. The contradictory

in European Communist and Fascist Cities since 1917 (Kimberly Elman Zarecor – Feruccio Trabalzi, orgs.), p. 71; Kimberly Zarecor, "Landscape of the Socialist Imagination: Reality and Unreality in the Construction of New Ostrava, Czechoslovakia," paper presented at the 8th EAUH Conference (Stockholm 2006), Session M15 The Socialist City – Concepts and Realities between Utopianism and Pragmaticism (Eliza Stanoeva – Nicole Münnich – Tanja Damljanović – Vladimir Kulić, orgs.), p. 7.

123 Béla Keregyártó, "The Present of the Recent Past: the Difficult Transformation of a 'Paradigmatic Socialist City.' The Case of Dunaújváros (Former Stalin City)," paper presented at the 9th EAUH Conference (Lyon 2008), Session S19, The Post-Socialist City: Continuity and Change in Urban Space and Imagery (Alfrun Kliems – Marina Dmitrieva, orgs.), p. 24.

124 Sonia Hirt, "Whatever Happened to the (Post)Socialist City?," *Cities* 32, Suppl. 1 (2013), p. 29.

nature of their design remains to be explained and understood: state planning with its prioritisation of industry gave origin to the monotony of housing, but also provided people with usable public spaces; the benefits of cheap communal services were often downplayed by poor provision; the appeal of immutable classical forms in socialist architecture coexisted with the deficit of and longing for the fashionable.

One of the most significant advancements visible in the intellectual production of the EAUH conferences is the revision of Socialist Realism that breaks through the "monolithisation" of the former socialist camp as regards its architectural practice. Seen in a broader historical context, we should better talk about the existence of socialisms in plural, with their versions dependent on the cultural context of the respective countries. The confines of the Cold War model of art history that prescribed to judge the matter of style on the basis of ideology were left behind. Rather than a divergence from the capitalist modernity, socialism shows itself as an idiosyncratic modern world.[125] Socialist modernity is the heir of European tradition, the implementation of which, however, took place in quite unique circumstances.

Another progress in recent historiography was the revision of the role of society in the life of cities. The socialist city was characteristic of shaping experiences from above, when identities were ascribed, and irresponsibility had developed in people relying on promises on the part of the power. And yet, people were also able to maintain their traditional outlook against new culture carried through by the power, and to rebel against the discipline of work and leisure. An urban reality emerged in the negotiations between power representatives and masses over the meaning of civility, comfort, and happiness. People reacted to discourses of power as active participants and not just as external observers, while their experiences were shaped by the ability of the power to define things on an official level.

Socialist cities are gone for good, but their legacy remains omnipresent in architecture and monuments and calls for re-interpretation. Although social reality has changed, the cities that were once socialist preserve their past not only in stone, but also in the thoughts of people who indeed remember the "rhythm of their steps." There is a task that stands in front of urban planners and urban historians: to help to work with these memories in a finer way when it comes to the shaping

---

125 Introduction to Session M37 Iron Curtain Cities? Urban Space in Cold War Europe (Moritz Fölmer – Marc B. Smith, orgs.), 12th EAUH Conference (Lisbon 2014).

of public spaces. The attitude to the past is an indicator of future development: similarly as the utopias of the previous centuries inspired the Avant-Gardists, the socialist past will be the subject of re-thinking, both in artistic and academic terms for generations to come.

Tractor at the Avenue: Post-War Reconstruction of Minsk, 1944-1960

Natallia Linitskaya

Introduction

When the first authentic model of tractors was produced at the Minsk tractor workshops in 1953, it rolled down the main avenue of recon-structed Minsk as a demonstration of the success of Soviet Belorussia.[126] A locomotive of progress, the red-coloured "Belarus," as the model was baptized, delivered "liberation to a country shackled with technical back-wardness," assisting the post-war restoration of order. The avenue led Belorussians to a "bright future" with cultural institutions, stores, and high schools, with architecture that was sound and beautiful; the tractor assured prosperity.

Destroyed in the Second World War, Minsk was reconstructed as a so-cialist city with a representative and "monumental" centre and industrial enterprises with housing estates for the employees and workers. Hous-ing in the socialist realist style with antique and art deco elements of decor provided an image of stability and happiness under Communism, while the social facilities of the socialist city were designed to support this promise in everyday life. This paper aims to explain socialist realist Minsk as a factor in the formation of Soviet Belorussian identity. Differ-ent views exist on the meaning of the reconstruction. The realization of the post-war master plan did not provide the city with a national form, the city was russified according to Thomas Bohn.[127] Some Belarusian

---

126 A note on the transcription: in the following text, the Soviet variant "Belorussia" and "Belo-russian" is used; contemporary names "Belarus" and "Belarusian" appear when related to the current state.

127 Thomas M. Bohn, *Minsk – Musterstadt des Sozialismus. Stadtplanung und Urbanisierung in der Sowjetunion nach 1945*, Köln: Böhlau 2008. For the account of the architectural debate on Stalin Avenue see pp. 94–105.

historians of architecture see the post-war style as a particular, local variation of Neoclassicism.[128] This article seeks to interpret the application of the traditional architectural language in Minsk as Sovietisation, the result of which Belorussians reasserted their nationhood, which was substantively connected with Sovietness. Since broad social support for the national "awakening" was not achieved prior to Sovietisation, it was Soviet national politics that formed Belorussians into a modern nation. Due to the late start of the national movement, people identified themselves as "Soviet" without "remembering" themselves as a nation prior to Sovietisation, the Soviet identity thus formed an integral part of Belarusian identity, stronger than in other Soviet republics. As Nelly Bekus explains, "...this Soviet formula of 'Belarusian-ness' was based on a combination of elements of socialist ideology, such as the egalitarian vision of social organization, with the institutional national form. Being 'Belarusian' in a Soviet way did not deny one's belonging to a larger Soviet community."[129]

The paper is based on two illustrative examples of reconstruction in correspondence with the main principles of Soviet urbanism: a spatially emphasized centre, and industrialization as the source of urban growth. In the first part, the plan of reconstruction of the centre and the stylistic expression are reinterpreted in relation to the cultural identity of Minsk. The second part checks the application of the plan to the example of an industrial neighbourhood, the housing settlement for employees of the tractor plant, which was a coherent realization of socialist realist garden-city design. The first part is based on secondary literature, but also on archival sources: the discussions of the Architectural Council by the Union of Architects of the BSSR that are located in the National Archive of Belarus (Nacionalnyj arkhiv Respubliki Belarus, NARB), fund 903, the Department for Architecture by the Council of Ministers of the

---

128 Alla Sergeevna Shamruk, *Arkhitektura Belarusi XX–XXI v.: Ehvoljucija stilej i khudozhestvennykh koncepcij* [The Evolution of Styles and Artistic Concepts], Minsk: Belorusskaja nauka 2007, p. 135.

129 Nelly Bekus, "'Hybrid' Linguistic Identity of Post-Soviet Belarus," *Journal on Ethnopolitics and Minority Issues in Europe* 13, no. 4 (2014), pp. 26–51, here p. 29. Accessible at: http://www.ecmi .de/fileadmin/downloads/publications/JEMIE/2014/Bekus.pdf. Insightful is also another study by Bekus, in which she applies the well-known three-phase (A–B–C) model of national movements, that was elaborated by Czech historian Miroslav Hroch, on the Belarusian case, with a fourth stage added, that is characterized as the institutionalisation of national culture under Socialism. See Nelly Bekus, "Nationalism and Socialism: 'Phase D' in the Belarusian Nation-Building," *Nationalities Papers* 38, no. 6 (2010), pp. 829–846. For the critique of the Hroch's model from the perspective of its application on Belarus, see p. 835.

BSSR (Upravlenije po delam arkhitektury pri Sovete Ministrov BSSR), as well as materials dealing with the construction of the tractor plant (fund 4 containing declassified files of KPB, the Communist party of Belorussia). The master plan was studied in the Belarusian State Archive of Scientific-Technical Documentation (Belorusskij gosudarstvennyj arkhiv nauchno-tekhnicheskoj dokumentacii, BGANTD, fund 3). The second part shows the preliminary results of research conducted in the archives of the tractor plant, located in the State Archive of Minsk district and the city of Minsk (Gosudarstvennyj arkhiv Minskoj oblasti i g.Minska, GAMO), where the tractor workshops agenda is collected in fund 3341. The cases discussed at the meetings of the workshops (fund 28) helped the understanding of everyday life in the settlement. Conversations with the residents of the site provided the author with both an impulse and material for understanding the popular identification with the Soviet legacy.

Provincial Town into Capital

Redesigned after the end of the Second World War, according to the understanding of representativeness suitable for the capital of a Soviet republic, the city did not restore its pre-war face, while its memory was also obliterated. The appearance of the new city concentrated by the central avenue combined classical expression in its administrative buildings with the pleasant panorama of residential housing and an abundance of greenery. In order to understand the meaning of reconstruction and the efficacy of a new image for Sovietisation, the past of Minsk should be hinted on.

Throughout the nineteenth century, the North-Western lands, an administrative unit in the Russian empire, were an agrarian region which lacked an urban centre that could play a unifying role in a cultural and economic sense. Minsk, one of the cities of Kievan Rus, was a node of trade on the route to Vilnius, Warsaw, and Moscow. By the mid-nineteenth century, it was a gubernatorial town with 23,000 permanent inhabitants plus a thousand foreigners. It had more Catholics than Orthodox members, and the Jewish population outnumbered members of both Christian denominations.[130] Polish and Russian cultural influenc-

---

130 Religion served as marker for ethnic belonging in the North-Western lands. Catholics were identified as Poles, while Orthodox with Russians or Belorussians. Uladzislaŭ Syrakomlja, *Minsk. Begły agljad suchasnaga stanu* [Minsk. A Quick Overview of the Current State], Minsk 1992 [1857], pp. 7–9.

Figure 3.1 The House of Government, 1930–1934. [Postcard]. The style is usually described as post-constructivist, meaning that the high quality of construction, monumentality and the art-deco motives are mixed here. The building formed an ensemble with a square in front of it and was meant to play a city-forming role. (Unknown photographer, 1961. A postcard from the collection of S. A. Prokopovich).

es, identified in the nineteenth century with either religion, were equally present in Minsk.

After the divisions of Poland at the end of the eighteenth century, Minsk was framed with a loyalty to the central Russian power, given a regular plan and classicist buildings in the centre. "From inside, the city of Minsk is defined with orderliness and order. The streets are broad and straight, the houses are not pressed next to each other, the air is clean... There is no crowd on the streets... the most important buildings are not shaded with others..."[131] The city centre – the Upper Town – was composed of a Baroque cathedral, completed by the Jesuits in 1710, and

<hr />

131 " Znutry mesta Minsk vyznachaecca akuratnascju i paradkam. Vulicy shyrokija i pramyja, damy zh ne scisnuty mizh saboju, pavetra chystae [...] Na vulicakh njama tlumu [...] budynki najbolsh vazhnaga znachehnnja ne zaslanjajucca inshymi..." Syrakomlja introduces Minsk in contrast to Vilnius, that still looked medieval, where history served the foundation for the development of national feelings. Ibid., p. 6.

a number of other churches and monasteries. To a Romantic poet, who travelled across the province in the mid-1850s, the place seemed provincial in a political sense, to which the absence of interest in theatre by Minskers was clearly a sign. The citizens of Minsk strolled in the Governor's garden – the first public park – discussing the cases in the courts but not politics.[132]

Minsk retained a provincial and multicultural profile, situated throughout the interwar decades on the "border between two worlds – USSR and the West," and yet it became the capital of Soviet Belorussia.[133] Of the 132,000 inhabitants in 1926 (the city began to grow due to the railroad construction in the last third of the nineteenth century), Belorussians made up 42%, Jews 40%, Russians 11%, and Poles 3%.[134] Soviet Belorussians could use any of four state languages, however, they felt no obligation to speak Belorussian – it was Russian which had the status of an urban language. In 1926, at the peak of Belorussianization, that is, establishing vernacular in education and bureaucratic domains, only half of the Belorussians of Minsk spoke in their native language.[135] About a third of the population earned their living independent of the state, 33% were state employees or students, and 20% workers.[136] In the play "Tutehjshyja" (literally "local people" or "locals", written in 1924), the national poet and writer Janka Kupala depicts Minsk borderland cultural identity with marginal social types and busy with trading. The main character tries to sell German currency at the moment when German troops are leaving the town, a scene alluding to the belatedness of Belorussians in creating a state of their own. The scene is set in the Upper Town (Market), continuing to be the city's historic forum.[137]

Nation-state building and modernist architecture overlapped in time. The campus for the State Belorussian University, opened in 1921, was built during the years 1928–31 in Constructivism (by I.K. Zaporozhec

---

132 Ibid., p. 13.

133 Cited in Ilja Kurkoŭ, *Minsk neznajomy, 1920–1940* [Minsk Unknown], Minsk: Uradzhaj 2002, p. 5.

134 Sachar Schybeka, "Das 'alte' Minsk: vom zarischen Gouvernementszentrum zur sowjetischen Hauptstadt," *Handbuch der Geschichte Weißrusslands*, Dietrich Beyrau – Rainer Lindner (eds.), Göttingen: Vandenhoeck & Ruprecht 2001, p. 314.

135 Steven L. Guthier, "The Belorussians: National Identification and Assimilation, 1897–1970," *Soviet Studies* 29, no. 1 (1977), pp. 37–61, here p. 53.

136 Schybeka 2001, p. 314.

137 The setting of the second act is "...a corner of Cathedral place, called by Minskers 'Braxalka'..." – literally a place, where one twaddles. Janka Kupala, "Tutehjshyja" [Locals]. *Poŭny zbor tvoraŭ* 7, Minsk: Mastackaja litaratura 2001, p. 286. The Upper Town was renamed Liberty Square under the Bolsheviks.

and G.L. Lavrov) together with a library (Lavrov, 1929–1932). The new way of public life was reinforced by the construction of new types of buildings, "fabrika-kitchen" (1936) and the club for food-industry workers (1929, A.K. Burov). The House of Government, followed by the House of the Red Army, the Opera and Ballet Theatre, and the Academy of Science (all designed by Iosif Langbard in 1929–1938) confirmed the construction of a nation-state. All of the buildings by Langbard survived the war and maintained their dominant position, being landmarks of socialist spatial organization to match the new society. The Belorussian intelligentsia did not survive – politicians, writers, poets, scientists, clergy were repressed in the 1930s.[138] However, the process of institutionalization of national culture did begin, and though it proceeded in Stalinist form, Belorussians were never doubted to be a nation.[139] But the variety of influences that fed Belorussian culture was reduced only to folk and Russian culture.

On the 3rd of July 1944, the Soviet army liberated Minsk from the German occupation that had lasted for three years. In total, 80% of the housing stock, along with the communal engineering and industrial substructure, was ruined. Wooden housing withstood the onslaught better while the central part of town suffered most. The panorama of walls and chimneys was striking, of the 700 stone buildings in the centre, some 200 survived, only a few dozen of which were later maintained.[140] From the 270,000 of Minsk inhabitants registered on the eve of the war, about 40,000 remained after the end of it.[141] Not only the demographic situation, but also the ethnic composition of Minsk changed radically as a result of the extermination of the Jews of Minsk (together with Jews deported from Western Europe to a Minsk ghetto). In the process of post-war urbanization, Minsk was populated with people from villages and other Soviet republics.

The goal that faced the Belorussian Government was to give Minsk a representative form of the capital of a Soviet republic that would ex-

138 Iryna Kashtaljan, "Belarus pad uplyvam palitychnykh rehprehsij saveckaga chasu (1917–1953)," *Mescy pamjaci akhvjaraŭ kamunismu ŭ Belarusi* [Places of Memory of the Victims of Communism in Belarus], Anna Kaminski (ed.), Leipzig: Fond dasledvannjaŭ kamunistychnykh dyktatur 2010, p. 15.

139 Bekus 2014, p. 35.

140 Vladimir Adamovich Korol – Aleksandr Petrovich Voinov – Evgenij Lvovich Zaslavskij et al., *Minsk. Opyt poslevojennoj rekonstrukcii i razvitija* [Minsk. Experience of the Post-War Reconstruction and Development], Moskva: Stojizdat 1966, p. 23.

141 Spartak Aleksandrovich Polskij, *Demografičeskie problemy razvitija Minska* [Demographic Problems of the Minsk Development], Minsk: Izdatelstvo BGU 1976, p. 11.

press both its weight in the Union, where it was third in terms of size, and recognition on the international arena, which BSSR acquired with a member voice in the United Nations thanks to the feats of the partisans. Belorussia as a Soviet Republic was a "younger sister" in respect to Russia and Ukraine, while as for the Belorussians themselves, this rhetoric spoke of promotion and security. War victimhood became a foundation-myth, in which the civil conflicts were never articulated, but the losses – the heaviest among European peoples and countries in the twentieth century[142] – were stressed again and again.[143] Its history began on an empty page and Belorussia, a country "dark and backward in the past" – another myth created to serve as the background to the socialist achievements – was granted a beautiful capital with heavy industry.

The famous Soviet architects Aleksej Shchusev, Arkadij Mordvinov, Nikolaj Kolli, Vladimir Semjonov, Boris Rubanenko, and professor Langbard were invited to Minsk in August 1944 to work on the layout of Minsk.[144] In the "sketch-idea" (ehskiz-ideja), provided by the commission in September 1944, the future centre was drafted, while the architects of the main planning institute, "Belgosprojekt," were entrusted with the elaboration of a master plan (Naum Trakhtenberg, who worked in Minsk before the war, played one of the leading parts). The city was reorganised on the basis of radial-ring system, the territory was doubled in size and zoned; a greenery of parks and boulevards fancied the city; suburbs and existing enterprises were removed from the centre; the territory by the river was gentrified; streets were broadened and straightened up and "one street overcoming all others in size and beauty, another, second in size crossing it, and a central square at the intersection of them" was envisioned as the central ensemble.[145]

This plan was based on the principles applied for the reconstruction of Moscow (Vladimir Semjonov, who consulted the architects in Minsk, was one of the authors of Moscow renovation in 1935), where the historic layout of the streets was maintained, but integrated functionally with transportation rings. The method rested in building along the main

142 Mikola Iwanou, "Terror, Deportation, Genozid. Demographische Veränderungen in Weißrussland in 20. Jahrhundert", *Handbuch der Geschichte Weißrusslands*, Dietrich Beyrau – Rainer Lindner (eds.), Göttingen: Vandenhoeck & Ruprecht 2001, p. 426.

143 Bernhardt Chiari, *Alltag hinter der Front. Besatzung, Kollaboration und Widerstand in Weißrussland 1941–1944*, Düsseldorf: Droste 1998. Chiari pointed out that the war caused the decomposition of Belorussian society due to the clashes of national and social identities.

144 Jurij Alekseevich Egorov, *Gradostroitelstvo Belorussii* [Urban Planning of Belorussia], Moskva: Gosudarstvennoje izdatelstvo literatury po stroitelstvu i arkhitekture 1954, p. 185.

145 Ibid., pp. 184, 186, 187.

arteries with façades turned to the street with an image that was meant to be joyful and optimistic. Ikonnikov explains how this vision was asserted: in 1934, when the plan of Moscow was under discussion, Stalin put together the stereotypical images of an ideal city with broad streets, beautiful squares, mighty green areas and full-flown rivers. The city was imagined as a piece of art, completed forever in ensemble and immutable form at the same time – a utopia which could be traced back to the Baroque city. Though the functional approach clearly underlined by the plan, real problems were secondary in relation to "aesthetical utopia".[146]

As for the style, the draft of Minsk made by the renowned team did not provide concrete instructions, only the size of the plots, the "red lines" observed for building in the corridor line, and the amount of flats were known.[147] Langbard, who supervised the elaboration of the plan by one of the workshops of "Belgosprojekt," defended the "beauty of construction," that is, adhered to constructivist interpretation of Socialist Realism, in which the rationality of construction was the main principle; Langbard wanted to "provide Belorussia with modern architecture."[148] His pre-war buildings would serve as an example as to style, while the House of Government built by him was considered to be an ideal of a new, essentially Soviet type of public architecture, remaining for a long time the biggest and the highest building in the Republic.[149] He faced objections from an emissary from the centre, Mikhail Osmolovskij, delegated to Minsk as Head of the Department for Architecture, an organ of control by the Council of Ministers of the BSSR.[150] Osmolovskij defended a pompous version of Socialist Realism.

"We say proudly that Sovetskaja Street in Minsk is Gorky Street in Moscow."[151] To Osmolovskij, who worked in Moscow when it was under reconstruction, a street had to be a showcase of socialist achievements: in the most exuberant manner it expressed the well-being and thus confirmed the legitimacy of the power. Gorky Street was built with massive residential houses with window-shops in the ground floors and was the

146 Andrej Vladimirovich Ikonnikov, Prostranstvo i forma v arkhitekture i gradostroitelstve [Space and Form in Architecture and Urban Planning], Moskva: KomKniga 2006, pp. 281–282.
147 NARB, f. 903, op.1, d. 92, l. 15.
148 BGANTD, a letter of Langbard to Osmolovskij, undated. Personal fund of Georgij Artemovich Parsadanov.
149 Anatolij Aleksandrovich Voinov, *I.G. Langbard*, Minsk 1976, p. 104.
150 NARB, f. 903, d. 92, l. 44. The Department for [the Issues of] Architecture was established by the Council of Ministers of USSR in 1942. The Belorussian Government had its own branch.
151 NARB, f. 903, op. 1, d. 92, l. 44. Pronounced at a meeting of the Architectural council, 14–15 February 1947.

realization of an idea of socialist superiority over political systems by reproducing a classic cultural example. In Minsk, the principle of "improvement" of space – a term common in the Soviet urban practice, referring to a solution of urban problems by aesthetical and technical elevation – was bound to the myth of overcoming local backwardness. In this case, constructivist, gubernatorial and Baroque architecture fell victim to the idea of beauty imagined to please generations of the future. According to the attitude "preserve, but radically reconstruct," value was ascribed to tradition only for the sake of confirmation of Socialist legitimacy in the world historical process, there was no care for saving specific objects.[152]

Osmolovskij insisted on the application of monumental classicist order for the residential buildings along the avenue. Belorussian artists (the plan for reconstruction was discussed by the whole artistic community) objected – as one of them put it: "Behind the columns, a man will be hidden."[153] The formula for socialist architecture was "socialist in content, national in form," and folklore ornamentations proliferated in the architecture of the Soviet republics. Saying that the "Belorussian Republic could not do without something of its own," they attempted to avoid administrative-like Classicism for residential purposes. But there was no clear alternative, as there was no local school of formal architecture to appeal to, only a feeling of cosiness expressed local spatiality as corresponding with the soft curves of the Minsk moraine hills and the provincial cultural climate.[154] Even if the attempts to provide "national form" did not expand further than using ornaments, the main achievement in this sense was retaining a scale that was not completely discontinuous with the pre-war city by avoiding gigantic forms, used in other Soviet cases, for example, Stalingrad. Minsk did not have the avenues of Eastern and Central Europe – Berlin, Warsaw, or Nowa Huta – where the modernist tradition adapted itself to the ideological expression and looked strict and massive.

The argument culminated in a discussion of a project of the Central Square which had been debated throughout 1947–48 (a closed compe-

---

152 Ikonnikov 2006, p. 283.

153 NARB, f. 903, op. 1, d. 92, l. 15.

154 National form in architecture is rooted in the mutual influence of culture, social order and political situation, and landscape. Regarding the social character of nature, historian of Russian literature Likhachev spoke of a "gentleness" of the Russian landscape, the natural curves of which were further softened by peasant cultivation. Dmitrij Sergeevich Likhachev, *Rodnaja zemlja* [Native Land], Moskva: Prosveshhenie 1983, p. 56. "The beauty lies not in monumentality, but in coziness" ("ujut"), said one of the Minsk architects. NARB, f. 903, op.1, d. 60, l. 68ob.

tition took place in May 1947). It was stated that Minsk did not have a "clearly defined centre with a public character," one of the key concepts for socialist realist urbanism that mirrored the political structure. Designed to be usable for demonstrations and army parades, a square was interpreted as having a political function; an example for this was found in the squares of Ancient Rome and Renaissance Italy. The place for the new square in Minsk was transposed only a few hundred meters away from the Upper Town, the tower-bell of the former Jesuit Cathedral was knocked down, erasing the provincial look and memory of the city. Langbard was against the new square as such, as one already existed in front of the House of Government. It was also clear that Minsk would have too many squares of too large a size, in which the city's population planned to reach half a million, and would be lost.[155] Osmolovskij insist-

Figure 3.2 Stalin Avenue with the People's Commissariat of State Security, NKGB, later KGB. [Postcard]. The building was realized in 1947 by Mikhail Parusnikov in due course of repressions against "rootless cosmopolitanism". The retrospective stylistic was used to support the idea of political unity between Russians and Belorussians. (Unknown photographer, the beginning of the 1960s, a postcard from the collection of S. A. Prokopovich).

155 NARB, f. 903, op.1, d. 60, ll 64ob–65, l. 76.

ed and proposed a colonnade with the statues of heroes, a pantheon.[156] None of the projects was realized. The competition consumed finances obtained for research into local housing for the elaboration of a typified series; a Baroque monastery of the Dominicans was not reconstructed.[157] Langbard was repudiated from the work in Minsk, and so was the pre-war interpretation of socialist architecture.[158]

By 1947, the first new building to be ready in Minsk was the "work of a master to whom the principles and methods of the Old Russian architects were a point of departure,"[159] the House of the NKGB, the Committee for State Security (architects Mikhail Parusnikov and Badanov). It occupied one block and defined not the style so much as the scale of the avenue. Parusnikov won the competition for the avenue in 1947 and designed the first line. Following the example of the Nevskij Prospekt in Saint-Petersburg, which served an etalon of ensemble, the avenue was as a corridor-street whose breadth (48 meters) corresponded with the height (five-seven floors), and the buildings were of similar size.[160]

The main avenue of Minsk acquired no high-rise buildings or esplanades; its scale was modest – according to the status of the third Soviet Republic as regards its size. The variation on Art Deco[161] elaborated by the Soviet architects was a stylistic expression working in harmony with both residential and cultural-administrative functions. The residential theme became major in the character of the avenue that was formed by blocks with inner yards. Arches connected houses, thus breaking the monotony of building in one line and framing entrances into the yards, in which the motive of balconies added domestic comfort to the simple network of windows, while the street façades were moulded as spectacular with the bow-windows; both impressiveness and comfort was achieved in this way. The plasticity of the façade walls, built up with standardized

156 NARB, f. 903, op. 1, d. 129, l. 75. One architect put straightforwardly that Osmolovskij's project did not have any artistic value. Ibid., l. 76.

157 NARB, f. 903, op. 1, d. 105, l. 182. From a budget of 510 thousand defined for typified urban planning, 370 thousand rubles was spent for the competition that took place on 15 May 1947.

158 NARB, f. 903, op. 1, d. 135, l. 208. The resolution "On Shortcomings in the Activity of the Soviet Socialist Architects" (18th August 1948) was a self-denouncing response of the Belorussian architects to the party repressions against culture known as *zhdanovshchina* (after the minister of culture Andrej Zhdanov). Egorov, the main architect of Minsk at that time, spoke against the designs by Langbard as "amerikanism". NARB, f. 903, op. 1, d. 129, l. 198.

159 Egorov 1954, p. 247.

160 A triumphal thoroughfare, the avenue was formed by the typified sections of houses. Ikonnikov 2006, p. 345. The sections were elaborated by Voinov, the head of the Union of Architects of BSSR, the branch of the all-union organization.

161 Bohn 2008, p. 96.

sections, was elaborated with pilasters, decorated with festoons, balustrades, and pediments. Even the functionalist buildings that survived acquired classicist details.[162]

Space was organized to appeal with facilities for cultured and healthy leisure. The first place completed in Minsk, the house of NKGB (People's Commissariat of State Security, Narodnyj komissariat gosudarstvennoj bezopasnosti), was designed in an ensemble containing a boulevard, fountain and benches. Its proportions created a human-scale space, despite being under the gaze of Feliks Dzerzhinskij, whose bust crowned the boulevard. Special emphasis was given to "dressing up the small but capricious river, the Svislach, into an embankment," which became a place for outings; and, the planting of parks – for the workers to enjoy the fresh air, the sun and greenery.[163] The warm tone of stucco – umber, ochre and terracotta – baskets and flowers in carefully cut compositions, the stone for plinths and the wood for door entrances were given careful consideration.

Greek and Italian motives were on view in the main buildings. Corinthean columns for the Palace of Culture of Trade Unions (architect V. Ershov, sculptors S. Selikhanov, A. Glebov, 1949–1954), a Palladian portico for the main post office (A. Dukhan, V. Korol, 1949–1953), Renaissance features for the state bank, a cupola for the circus set amidst the greenery of parks.[164] Everything that represented Belorussia as a socialist state was concentrated at the avenue, the whole city packed into one line. Decorated space engulfed a worker strolling along the avenue; by pleasing and uplifting aesthetically, it had to raise in him and her the feeling of patriotic and moral duty, at the same time, to form the attitude of the flaneur, since everything one could imagine under the word "civilization" or "culture" or "progress," was right in front of one's eyes.[165] The architect had to feel responsibile and be a "statesman" as it were.[166] As for the citizens, the Belorussians-from-huts liked the Belorussia risen-high-in-stone.[167]

---

162 Aleksandr Petrovich Voinov, *Zhilishchnoe stroitelstvo v Belorusskoj SSR* [Housing Construction in the Belorussian SSR], Minsk 1980, p. 60.

163 Egorov 1954, pp. 186–187.

164 Shamruk 2007, pp. 136–137.

165 Katerina Clark points that a soviet citizen of the 1930's was expected to become a flaneur who wanders along the parade streets of socialist city in order to absorb "visual impressions." See her *Moscow, the Fourth Rome: Stalinism, Cosmopolitanism and the Evolution of Soviet Culture, 1931–1941*, Cambridge, Mass. – London: Harvard University Press 2011, p. 103.

166 The architect's role as "creator" ('zodchij') was applied to Stalin himself. See ibid., p. 92.

167 A paraphrase of a poem about Moscow: "Old ones and small ones // are looking at bronze and stone, – // That's how in proud astonishment // Russia looks at itself." Boris Sluckij, "Tolpa na Teatralnoj ploshchadi" [Crowd on the Theater square], Leningrad: Izdatelstvo TsK VLKSM "Molodaja gvardija" 1965, pp. 18–19.

Figure 3.3 Palace of Culture of Trade Unions. [Postcard]. A socialist realist variation of Antique temple decorated with statues representing socialist labourers, among them a Peasant-Woman, a Worker, a Sportsman, a Musician and a Scientist. The palace became a target for the critique within the new architectural paradigm under Khrushchev that saw it as old-fashioned and expensive. (Unknown photographer, the beginning of the 1960s, a postcard from the collection of S. A. Prokopovich).

The windows of GUM, the state department store, adorned with sheaves of wheat and figures of dancers in folk costumes, signaled national prosperity. Achieving it, Belorussian peasants became a socialist nation: what they, "backward and uncultured," were deprived of in the past, became available under Socialism; national identity was built up on the basis of socialist myth. That is why the grand store was nowhere else but at the main avenue, while the small shops of artisans and traders, traditional for Minsk, were hidden from view until they disappeared in the second phase of reconstruction. A Russian example played the role of classic tradition; its appropriation proved that Belorussians mastered high culture and played equal part in the unity of nations. The decorative role of the vernacular was demonstrated in the folk ornament on the tomb under the statue of Stalin, standing on Central Square from 1952 till 1961. Belorussians occupied an "honourable place amidst nations," being a member of the family of Eastern Slavs: "Along our broad streets

I will walk // My city is in the constellation of fraternal capitals."[168] The country existed proudly in this fraternal union.

The reconstruction of Minsk was defined by the need to transform the city of its provincial look and borderland identity into a Soviet capital. The architectural representation of Soviet Belorussia could have become modernist with its strict "beauty of construction", as it was proposed by Langbard, but instead a softer and more traditional character was asserted by the central power. In housing, Art Deco elements were combined with classicist ones, Greek order prevailed in the administrative examples. Belorussian national identity was realized in a form that could be understood as more submissive if to think of a potential effect that could be achieved by modernist, more ascetic forms, and also more provincial – a province that acquired representative architecture. However, to speak about Russification would not be accurate; it rather fixed the existing consciousness of cultural and political unity with Russia, but emphasized it in one-sided manner. Apprehensive, as Russian Classicism was a part of the historical tissue of the city, Stalin Avenue embodied the idea of statehood, which Belorussians lacked in history, playing in this way the role of an "invented tradition," in the sense of the concept coined by Eric Hobsbawm.

There was also a socialist pillar under new Minsk. With its beauty and sound, the avenue became a guarantee that the poverty experienced in the past of this nation would not repeat itself in the future. The expectation of prosperity was the foundation of social cohesion of the Belorussians, who, in the case of the citizens of Minsk, represented a more homogenous entity when compared with the pre-war multiethnic population. Though the layout of the city expressed loyalty, the proportionality of the buildings on the avenue, together with its human scale and the quality of its space ensured that Minsk remained a liveable city.

Tractor-Builders are Searching for Urbanity

In this section we will explore the social space of a working neighbourhood of Minsk with a variety of cultural and social facilities to be used as tools for forging Soviet citizens. Before we have a look at the tractor-builders, it is useful to remember that their neighbourhood appeared

---

168 Anatol Veljugin, "Dvorec Pionerov" [The Palace of Pioneers], in: *Molodaja Belarus* [Young Belarus], Leningrad: Izdatelstvo TsK VLKSM "Molodaja gvardija" 1952, p. 45.

in the background of a large social transformation connected with urbanization and industrialization, in which the small-scale and manufac-
ture-like character of Belorussian industry was completely transformed
and the working force from the countryside teamed to job positions
opening in the heavy industry. It may well be assumed, with reference to
similar situations in other socialist countries, that the abundance of labour reserves was one of the reasons for the Belorussian model of socialist transformation to become successful.[169] This macroeconomic factor
was supported by the desire of people to achieve a life better than it was
possible in moneyless collectivized villages, the *kolkhozes*.

The tractor construction site was founded in May 1946 and held the
status of all-union importance.[170] Its neighbourhood was supposed to
become the core of a large industrial district.[171] It was designed as a garden-city – an idea that fit socialist urbanism as healthful and culturally
improving. There was the need to make space functional and self-contained, and the socialist realist architectural trend underlined design as
a "settlement." It had two secondary schools and a music school, a public
bath, policlinics, a sports stadium and, naturally, a club with a cinema,
a dozen shops, several cafeterias and a number of canteens – all to be
completed by the end of the 1950s or the beginning of the 1960s at the
latest. It was separated from the workshops with a green belt, connected
to the city by a tram line. Detached and self-sufficient, this space developed an idiosyncratic semi-urban, semi-peripheral culture of living.

The socialist city was claimed to have no periphery, that is, the standard of housing and services available for the workers was of the same
quality as that in the city centre. But the periphery was simpler: houses
were lower, the décor of the walls less elaborated.[172] Construction began
with the inner blocks; small units of eight flats were built during 1946–
1949. By 1950–1955, three-story structures in the same blocks were ready.
A representative housing complex with *cours d'honneur* was finished by
1957–59. The houses on Dolgobrodskaja street leading to the centre were
designed in 1961, altogether fourteen blocs with vast inner courtyards.
By the beginning of the 1960s, construction of five-story block and panel
housing on the edges of the settlement was organized on the basis of

169 For this argument applied to other socialist countries, see Dagmar Jaješniak-Quast, *Stahlgigant-
en in der sozialistischen Transformation: Nowa Huta in Krakau, EKO in Eisenhüttenstadt und Kunčice
in Ostrava*, Wiesbaden: Harrassowitz 2010, p. 102.
170 NARB, f. 4, op. 29, d. 838, l. 2.
171 NARB, f. 903, op. 1, d. 135, l. 119.
172 Shamruk 2007, p. 150.

a cooperative. The last building constructed according to the original plan was the House of Culture (1965): planned as first, it came last and in a modernist shape.

The tractor-builders' main square was marked with a high-rise, while back streets were composed of smaller structures according to the hierarchy of space in the socialist realist ensemble. The plan organized space so that it would be easy for the inhabitants to orient themselves and for the authorities to control. The settlement was intersected by a boulevard that went to the factory gates, and another street, Stakhanovskaja, ran throughout the area crossing the boulevard; these two streets were the cords of public life, while others were quiet, of residential character. Streets, crossing one another at right angles, creating perspectives and stressed at the corners with towers, achieved a mood in line with the public space and its distinctive personality, complemented by the atmosphere of the yards.

The perimetric construction created inner yards that were specific micro spaces where social control and the intimacy of neighbourhood life intertwined. Blocks were built to a modest height, and the atmosphere there was semi-private. Such a yard contained traditional objects, such

Figure 3.4 The tractor workshops neighborhood, a courtyard. Chatting on a bench by a house belongs to everyday culture of the neighborhood. (Photo by Igor Korzun, 2015).

as a shed for animals or wood for heating the ovens, wooden toilets, and facilities for spending free time: tables, benches. On the edges of the settlement, there were plots where people grew potatoes – a normal part of living in the city as help in the hungry post-war years. The plots were given by the trade union committees to the families of the employees. Young people singing and dancing to the accordion (*harmonika*), children playing a *cossacks vs. bandits* game, fathers playing dominos, housewives chatting or taking care of hens, rabbits or even a piglet in the sheds – such was the social life inside the blocks. Skating rinks, dancing floors, and football pitches left imprints of happiness in the memories of the inhabitants.

There is no surprise that the residents who had been children in the 1950s–1960s stressed that they enjoyed their time spent playing games and exploring different adventures: the settlement with a suburban character and remnants of forests and a river as one of its frontiers provided them with the pleasure of being close to nature; besides, the ground floors of the small-type units opened directly onto the grass in the summer and snow in the winter.[173] Hygiene and health were a matter of control, so trees were planted and even fountains made in the most fashionable blocs. In addition to the greenery inside the blocs, the settlement had several parks. Everyone claimed to enjoy their eleven square metres of greenery per capita; children sunbathed on the verandas of the kindergartens.[174] Healthcare for everyone remained on paper, though. A plead for improving housing conditions dated 1950 and written by a widow of an officer stated: "My children are prevented from properly using their summer vacations, being stopped by the factory gate each time they leave and return home."[175] That family of five people lived in a mud hut on the territory of the plant.

How were the discrepancies of socialist living perceived by people? The years spent in the barracks are remembered differently by people from different social groups: by those of higher position as having temporary inconveniences that did not matter a lot, without too much attention, as if it were mere curiosities denounced for striking the imagination of the interviewer: both hardships and the following improvement was perceived as given.[176] The possible explanation lies not only in the social

---

173 Conversations with Tatjana Butenko, June 2013; Tatjana Rogovenko, November 2015.
174 GAMO, f. 3341, op. 1, d. 45, l. 46; 18 m² in the centre. Korol et al. 1966, p. 25. The average amount of living area was 2–4 m² per person.
175 GAMO, f. 3341, op. 1, d. 1117 (the protocols of a work shop trade union committee), ll. 189–189 ob.
176 Conversations with Zinaida Alekseevna Shershneva, May 2013; Lidija Ivanova, May 2013.

Figure 3.5 A house on Stakhanovskaja street, renovated. The ground-floor veranda was bricked and turned into a room, a common tactic of the tenants in the 1970s and 1980s. (Photo by Igor Korzun, 2015).

status of the respondents, but in the circumstances of their arrival to the site: people who came first, when each pair of hands was valued and especially trained, or professionals, felt welcomed. Those who came to the city later, in the 1950s–1960s, remember initial hardships as humiliating, while the moment of receiving a flat meant both a fulfilled promise given by the state and individual luck and was indeed valuable.[177] One should notice the fact that the newcomers of the Khrushchev time came to the city explicitly for the opportunities of urban life, while the first settlers thought of physical survival and social anchoring. In both cases, ideology participated in the organization of memories: in the first case, it was the Stalinist "care about man", in the second it was "satisfying the material needs of toilers."

To create a coherent impression and propagate the idea of social equality, the settlement was planned to be built along standardized lines of 8, 16, and 24 flats. Despite the call to use one series only, several in fact were applied.[178] The design of the two-story houses was simple, the decor

177 Conversation with Zinaida Ivanovna, August 2013.
178 NARB, f. 903, op. 1, d. 135, ll. 118–119.

optimistic and energetic. At the same time, wooden verandas alluded to peaceful family well-being, while storage rooms built into the flats aimed at household sufficiency. A mixture of bow-windows, French balconies, rosettes and vases painted a "lyric and friendly" picture.

Most of the series were designed with isolated rooms, which presupposed the occupation of the flats by rooms, while hallway and bathrooms were used as additional places to sleep, work or play.[179] To obtain even one room when the settlement was under construction gave reasons for happiness. One resident recalled the moment of acquiring a flat: "August afternoon [we] ran there, holding hands; the flat was lit up by the sun and smelled of fresh wood and paint."[180] So the identifying narrative proceeds, unifying individuals and space. For families of valued cadres, flats and rooms were given individually; the fact of living in a flat of one's own was a distinguishing characteristic. For unqualified youths, the settlement showed another side, one of overcrowded dormitories and a lack of amenities. Barracks, cold and damp, were in use until 1962 and accommodated over five hundred people.[181]

By the beginning of the 1950s, the settlement embodied urban life. Though quite modest in comparison with the scale of such Central European urban socialist sites as Nowa Huta or Ostrava-Poruba, the settlement of the tractor-builders, nicknamed "Little Paris," was fashionable when contrasted with the barracks and even more so with the countryside. The *gastronom* (food store) could boast of better supplies than those normally available. Shop windows bulged with jars of caviar and a wide range of sausages, which were pleasing the wealthier ones and stimulating poor young trainees to make careers, while widows and invalids shared the feeling of despair and resentment when looking at unaffordable food. However, individual resentment did not transform into organized protest against the plant and party authorities. The groups of workers wandering without work indeed terrified the authorities at the beginning of plant construction.[182] However, the chances for rebellious moods to become collective action did not realize. The reasons for this

---

179 Conversation with Lidija Ivanova, May 2013.
180 Remembered by Jelena Stepanovna Smirnova, who moved into a newly-built house in 1950, where her family occupied one room in a two-room flat. Conversations throughout 2012–2015.
181 GAMO, f. 3341, op. 1, d. 1129, l. a.
182 Helplessness of the party against the "tranquility and ignorance" of the people-in-charge of the workshops which caused resentment of the workers can be read throughout the protocols of the party cell in the initial postwar period. There were not enough machines to work on, no place to live, no medical care. The situation with workers as "desperate" was described by a meeting of the party bureau in the beginning of 1947. GAMO, f. 28(n), op.1, d. 12. l. 16.

are the following: a desire to perform well was not rare, as the youth was curious for technique and thirsty for work, interested in being accepted into the working collective, and so the success of the plant quickly became a matter of one's concern; on the other hand, drudgery consumed the time and strength of the veterans with their health destroyed during the war; drinking was the way how to react to different offenses. At the same time, the majority of people lived very modestly, and an image of how a festive dinner looks like – herring and potatoes – was shared by all strata, while the youth enveloped the atmosphere of settlement with hopes for the future.[183]

The need to look like urbanites, to possess and to demonstrate signs of an urban lifestyle, was marked amongst various categories of newcomers, and thus the settlement that appeared on green grass was extremely prone to an appropriation of Soviet culture as urban life style. Young people, who arrived from the villages, and also those who had their social status thrown into confusion by the war, did their best to acquire an urban look. Those who moved from other republics and were afraid of losing their cultural and social identity supported Soviet urban lifestyle as securing respectability. In the nationally diverse space of communal flats, Belorussians, Ukrainians, and Jews were becoming working class, learning skills and urban attire, but retaining national identities too, which were used for more subtle social stratification.[184] In a story about the neighbour who hung out her slip for drying in a communal kitchen so that everyone could appreciate her "cultured-ness," her nationality was bound to her social origin: Belorussian equalled bumpkin.[185] Belorussians followed an urban life-style not only in fashion but also soon had their children attending Russian schools. In 1960, the studying of the Belorussian language became non-obligatory and was in fact not learned in the settlement school, which was named after Russian writer A.P. Chekhov.[186] Those who did not consider themselves as Belorussians

---

183 Conversation with Lidija Ivanova, May 2013.

184 The specialists were invited from other Soviet republics and enjoyed priority in provision with flats. This supported stratification of the tractor-builders' society along national identities which, in the eyes of the people themselves, were linked to social status. GAMO, f. 3341, op. 1, d. 1210 (The file contains orders issued by the vice-director of the plant responsible for *byt*, that is, housing and everyday life), l.73.

185 The Belorussian origin of the girl was emphasized by her Ukranian neighbour. Conversations with Jelena Stepanovna Smirnova, undated, throughout 2012–2015.

186 Valencin Genrykhavich Mazec, "Transfarmacyjnyja pracehsy ў sitehme shkolnaj adukacyi Minska (1945-1990)," *Minsk i Minchane. Dzesjac stagoddzjaў gistoryi*, Minsk: Belaruskaja navuka 2010, p. 206.

Figure 3.6 Stakhanovskaja street around 1950, houses just completed (by architect V. N. Kostenko). The picture shows a street scene in the vicinity of the food store and a shop in which textile was sold, one of the most attractive places for men and women of the neighbourhood. (Courtesy of Belorusskij gosudarstvennyj arkhiv nauchno tekhnicheskoj dokumentacii, f. 51, op. 1, d. 301, l. 10 a).

were allowed to omit Belorussian, although the subject as such did not disappear from the school curriculum.

A sign of modernity was the pharmacy located in the fanciest house on the square. While the sewing-room could barely satisfy demand, private tailors flourished.[187] Jackets, slightly oversized on the girls' shoulders, and if worn along with an embroidered blouse, represented modernity, which was displayed by young people from the countryside and at the same time forming them. Perms, watches and lipstick were unimaginable in the village but to be seen in the settlement. In a suit, in a dress and hat, one promenaded along the Tractor-builders' Boulevard, watched fireworks in the evening or went to listen to a concert in the Pioneer park. Tractor-builders aspired to a cultured life – young

---

187 Conversations with Jelena Stepanovna Smirnova. Mentioned throughout 2012–2015.

girls escaping their villages rushed to the library for books, if only once or twice, before marrying and being quickly overtaken by households, young fathers spent free time playing football with their trade union teams as a relaxation from family life. Despite the fact that rank-and-file tractor-builders remained uninvolved in public life, being satisfied with occasional movies and dancing parties, they became Soviet citizens precisely by practicing this routine.

Immediately after the war, to move to a city was a matter of survival. With the take-off of industrialization on the one hand and the scarcity of money in the villages on the other, moving to the city became appealing, especially to young people. The motivation to become a skilled worker was understandable – the plant promised housing in the city, career prospects and related perquisites, while *kolkhozes* provided practically no money. The plea of a poet "Do not call my country the land of forests // Look, factory lights are shining above it" was made when electric lights, chemical fertilizers and tractors were only being introduced or reintroduced into Belorussian *kolkhozes*.[188] Spatiality of the neighbourhood did not arise on the basis of decisions from above exclusively, but was formed in the attitude of the people who appropriated ideas of urban life-style such as cultured leisure or fashionable garments, to places delimited by the official discourse. Space and people underwent the process of evolvement together, as a result of which people identified themselves with Soviet urbanity, while the place experienced the formative influence of the traditional habits of the settlers.[189]

---

188 Kastus Kirehenka, "Moja Respublika" ("Ne zovite moju respubliku stranoju tjomnykh lesov, // Posmotrite, nad neju svetjatsja ogni zavodskikh korpusov...") Molodaja Belarus. Sbornik stikhov belorusskikh poehtov [Young Belarus. The Collection of Verses by Belorussian Poets], Leningrad: Izdatelstvo Komsomola 1952, pp. 7–13.

189 Thomas Bohn sees in the process of rapid urbanization of Minsk the traits of ruralization. See his "Von jüdischen Schtetln zu sowietischen Industriestädten. Paradoxien der Urbanisierung Weißrusslands," *Von der "europäischen Stadt" zur "sozialistischen Stadt" und zurück? Urbane Transformationen im östlichen Europa des 20. Jahrhunderts*, Thomas M. Bohn (ed.), München: Oldenburg Verlag 2009, pp. 51–76. Felix Ackermann interprets the process of urbanization of Belarus as Sovietisation, that is, constructing of specific Soviet urban culture, and this seems to be a more accurate explanation. See, for example, his "Savetyzacyja i pamjac. Transnacyjanalnaja pamjac pra stalinskija rehprehsii ŷ Zakhodnjaj Belarusi?" [Sovietisation and Memory. Transnational Memory of the Stalinist Repressions in Western Belarus?], Mescy pamjaci akhvjaraŷ kamunizmu ŷ Belarusi [Places of Memory of the Victims of Communism in Belarus], Anna Kaminski (ed.), Leipzig: Fond dasledvannjaŷ kamunistychnykh dyktatur 2010, pp. 75–84.

Conclusion

Reconstruction in the late Stalinist period should be regarded as the creation of capitals and thus related to the nation-state policy of the Bolsheviks. To understand it as Russification is not precise since there was nothing clearly "national" about Minsk prior to the "zero hour," neither was there a coherent architectural school. The dispute between Langbard, who was based in Leningrad and approached Socialist Realism as a Constructivist, and Osmolovskij with his traditionalist views, was "a battle over styles," a collision of interpretations of Socialist Realism. It resulted in a compromise variant, in which tranquillity of the classicist image corresponded with the historic scale of Minsk. Such a city appealed as it encompassed a promise of comfortable life expressed through beautiful walls and interiors of the shops, parks and facilities for entertainment. The tempo of the growth of Minsk, the highest among the cities of the same size, proved that Minsk played the role of a "state condenser" thanks to the architecture, facilities and the offer of working places.[190]

The settlement of the tractor-builders replicated the scheme of the central ensemble and despite its peripheral location, its inhabitants accepted the same values as those translated through the central ensemble. These were beauty, comfort, domesticity and self-improvement. It was their motives for moving, endurance when waiting for a room, and above all their everyday routine that identified the tractor-builders as Soviet citizens. The young of the 1950s, once they moved to the capital from the villages, became urbanites as inhabitants of a self-contained garden-city. The appropriation of Soviet urbanity was mediated by the communication between various social strata, cultural and ethnic identities, which, contesting over the access to the places and cultural facilities controlled and distributed from above, participated in the formation of the settlement. Without moving out, or changing their place of work, the generation born in the 1920s and 1930s retained the values of honour of work and an appreciation of domesticity that were engendered by post-war conditions and further reinforced by the spatial structures of the neighbourhood.

So how deeply did Belorussians adopt Soviet identity? Only preliminary conclusions may be drawn on the basis of the situation in the

---

190 Polskij 1976, pp. 12–16. Polskij conceived of the definition "Minsk phenomenon" describing the fastest growing tempo among the cities of similar size particularly due to migration from the hinterland.

tractor-builders' settlement as the ambiguity of the attitudes of various groups makes the task complicated at this stage of research. It is clear that the combination of the devastation from the war, the economic course of the country, plant paternalism, and people's wishes, all served as the foundation for the positive perception of the regime or, to put it in other words, adherence to the socialist promise. The difficulty of further clarifying this attitude which could consist of approval and disapproval on various occasions lies in the lack of manifestations of the beliefs by the people themselves. At the same time, silence was speaking for itself and was historically and culturally characteristic of Belorussians. It seems that the co-existence of the people and the socialist regime was a venture convenient for both sides, and to such a degree that the inertia of consent is apprehensive even nowadays.[191] The process of rapid growth that took place in the 1960s and the following decades, and during which the image and content of the city was changing in an even more dramatic way than during the socialist realist phase, remains beyond the limits of this chapter. The modernist phase of post-war reconstruction under Khrushchev strongly contributed to the formation of Belorussian Soviet outlook, while a Stalinist city and identity continued to serve as the foundation to people's Soviet identity.

---

191 The author draws on the notion of Victoria de Grazia concerning the methodological "futility"of searching for "authentic" opinion of people in the conditions of an authoritarian regime which "[...] as long as it had some degree of cooperation, was perfectly satisfied with silence, no matter whether this masked indifference or disapproval." See her *The Culture of Consent. Mass Organization of Leisure in Fascist Italy*, Cambridge: Cambridge University Press 2002, p. 20.

Public Spaces and Nation-Building in Post-Soviet Kazakhstan (1991-2001)

Nari Shelekpayev

Introduction

This chapter explores public spaces in two cities: Almaty, the former capital of Kazakhstan, and Astana, the country's current capital. Specifically it looks at *Respublika Alany* (Republic Square) in Almaty, and the left bank of the Ishim river in Astana.[192] Despite losing its status as a capital city, Almaty continues to play an important role in the country's economic and cultural life. Astana, founded in the nineteenth century, acquired a new identity after 1997. It is sometimes called an advertising project for Kazakhstan's authorities. This study provides a partial analysis of the post-socialist transformation of the above-mentioned public spaces, based on the study of architects and sculptors' works, history textbooks, and a corpus of graphic representations.

A number of scholars questioned the issues related to the relocation of the capital city from the south to the north,[193] the relationship between the political landscape in Kazakhstan and its capitals' cityscape,[194]

---

192 This text stems from a chapter of my M. A. thesis, entitled "Kazakh Capitals and the Construction of Kazakh National Identity, 1991–2011," which I defended at the École des Hautes Études en Sciences Sociales de Paris in June 2013. I would like to thank Prof. Luďa Klusáková (Charles University in Prague), Prof. Nancy M. Wingfield (Northern Illinois University), and Dr. Jaroslav Ira (Charles University in Prague) who read and commented on this paper several times.

193 Henry R. Huttenbach, "Whither Kazakstan? Changing Capitals: From Almaty to Aqmola/ Astana," *Nationalities Papers* 26, no. 3 (1998), pp. 581–596; Richard L. Wolfel, "North to Astana: Nationalistic Motives for the Movement of the Kazakh(Stani) Capital," *Nationalities Papers* 30, no. 3 (2002), pp. 485–506. Edward Schatz, "What Capital Cities Say about State and Nation Building," *Nationalism and Ethnic Politics* 9, no. 4 (2004), pp. 111–140.

194 Natalie Koch, "The Monumental and the Miniature: Imagining 'Modernity' in Astana," *Social & Cultural Geography* 11 (2010), pp. 769–787; Adrien Fauve, "L'architecture d'Astana : Her-

the construction of national identity and tensions between its civic and ethnic forms in post-Soviet Kazakhstan,[195] the role of Kazakhstan's elites in the nation-building process,[196] the social effects of the built environment in Astana,[197] and so on. These works mainly focused on the protagonists of the nation-building process and their techniques for the transformation and development of space, while the appropriation and instrumentalisation of time for nation-building purposes received less attention. This chapter aspires to fill this gap and demonstrates that the material construction of post-Soviet "kazakhness" was characterized by a primordialist appeal to the past in the case of Almaty, while for Astana it was based on a detachment from the past and the imaginary appropriation of a desired future through a grandiose modernist project. Grasping this process may contribute to seeing the relocation of the capital city as part of a broader nation-building process, rather than solely a politically generated discontinuity. Ultimately, it may also help in rethinking the complex nature of nation-building in post-Soviet Kazakhstan, whose main protagonists were its major cities, Almaty and Astana.

Constructing National Identity: Actors and Techniques

The term "national identity" is ambiguous, and sometimes confusing.[198] This text proceeds from the assumption that identity does not have immutable, innate characteristics. Rather, it is constructed by different actors in constant interaction and negotiation with one another. Until the mid-1980s the notion of "kazakhness" was not manifest in public

méneutique d'une néo-capitale," *Patrimoine et architecture dans les états post-soviétiques*, Taline Ter-Minassian (ed.), Rennes: Presses universitaires de Rennes 2013.

195 Bhavna Dave, *Kazakhstan. Ethnicity, Language and Power*, London – New York: Routledge 2007; Donnacha Ó Beacháin – Rob Kevlihan, "Threading a Needle: Kazakhstan between Civic and Ethno-Nationalist State-Suilding," *Nations and Nationalism* 19, no. 2 (2013), pp. 1–20.

196 Sally N. Cummings, "Legitimation and Identification in Kazakhstan," *Nationalism and Ethnic Politics*, 12, no. 2 (2006), pp. 177–204.

197 Victor Buchli, "Astana: Materiality and the City," *Urban Life in Post-Soviet Asia*, Catherine Alexander – Victor Buchli – Caroline Humphrey (eds.), London – New York: University College London Press 2007, pp. 40–69; Alima Bissenova, "The Master Plan of Astana: Between the 'Art of Government' and 'the Art of Being Global,'" *Ethnographies of the State in Central Asia: Performing Politics*, Madeleine Reeves – Johan Rasanayagam – Judith Beyer (eds.), Bloomington – Indianapolis: Indiana University Press 2014, pp. 127–148.

198 See Rogers Brubaker, "Myths and Misconceptions in the Study of Nationalism," *The State of the Nation: Ernest Gellner and the Theory of Nationalism*, John A. Hall (ed.), Cambridge: Cambridge University Press 1998, pp. 272–305.

discourse. As for "identity," the Kazakh language does not yet have a precise analogue of this term.[199] In the 1980s, spontaneous discourses on national consciousness and self-determination began to emerge but the nationalistic claims were often reduced to ethnic or linguistic issues directed outward (*who is the other?*), and less to someone's proper identity (*who am I?*).[200] At the same time, the republican government faced these claims with suspicion: on the one hand, nationalistic movements gained strength and could not be ignored without prejudice to the integrity of the Soviet State; on the other hand, the majority of people, and part of the elite, had a strong desire to keep the Union as a powerful supranational structure.[201]

The situation changed after 1991, when state authorities institutionalized a top-down search for a national idea and the fabrication of its respective representations. A new flag, coat of arms, currency, and territorial reforms were inspired and sponsored by Kazakhstan's government and sequentially introduced during the 1990s.

Language and schools are considered as being among the most important instruments of state ideology.[202] However, both language policy and school education are providers rather than manufacturers of this ideology: they can transmit certain ideas and symbols only if these already exist. Even though a major political shift occurred in 1991, portraits of Lenin and the Soviet Union's coat of arms on letters of commendation disappeared from classes only around 1994–1995. As for rituals, such as the obligatory listening to the national anthem, and "made-in-Kazakhstan" tutorials, they were introduced across-the-board in the late 1990s, almost ten years after Kazakhstan's independence.

Language is often mentioned in conjunction with schools. The role and status of the Kazakh language in post-Soviet Kazakhstan have increased significantly since 1991. Giulia Panicciari pointed out that according to official statistics, in 2009–2010 the total number of secondary school students studying in the Kazakh language throughout the

199 The closest Kazakh expression corresponding to the English word "identity" is birdeilik uksatyk [бірдейлік ұқсастық], but this cannot be considered a full synonym for the term and the notion of "identity," such as is implied in this research.
200 This is not to say that such discourse did not exist before 1980. Rather I suggest that it took, after 1980, a particular articulation that is further explored in this article.
201 See the results of the 1990 all-union referendum.
202 See Miroslav Hroch, "From National Movement to Fully-formed Nation," *New Left Review* 198, no. 1 (1993), pp. 3–11; Miroslav Hroch, "National Self-Determination from a Historical Perspective," *Canadian Slavonic Papers / Revue Canadienne des Slavistes* 37, no. 3/4 (1995), pp. 283–299.

country was one and a half million, whereas for Russian the number was only 870,000. In Almaty, the majority of secondary schools still taught in Russian at that time. For Astana and many other cities the situation is quite similar even today. Naturally, the issue is not in which language one is being taught since an ideology can be transmitted in any language. However, Kazakh officials made speeches in Russian, and a considerable part of the press was printed in Russian as well. Kazakhstan's president wrote about the role of the Kazakh language in 2003:

> "We need to be realistic and understand that today only political values can rally us. Although such a cultural integrator as the Kazakh language should certainly play a more significant role, the afterburner by way of forging a single ethnic consciousness for all Kazakhstan's people may turn to be a tragedy."[203]

Thus, neither school education nor linguistic "kazakhisation" were sufficient for providing a satisfactory content for the national idea. A transformation of existent public spaces in order to fill them with new symbolic content and a construction of such new spaces that would visually incarnate different political values (and require a more concerted effort by fewer actors) became an alternative nation-building tool. One such attempt was undertaken in Almaty. However, it was the construction of a new governmental district in Astana and its adjacent territories that became the most successful endeavor for mobilizing the public imagination through actual construction, media promotion, guided tours, and so on.

Republic Square in Almaty: an Appropriation of the Past

In the introduction to "Power and Landscape" W. J. T. Mitchell claimed that landscape "naturalizes a cultural and social construction, representing an artificial world as if it were simply given and inevitable, and it also makes that representation operational by interpolating its beholder in some more or less determinate relation to its givenness as sight and site."[204] In light of this double role, distinguished by Mitchell, the example of Almaty's Republic Square is evocative since it provides a charac-

---

203 Nursultan Nazarbayev, *In the Stream of History*, Almaty: Atamura 2003, p. 182.
204 W. J. T. Mitchell, "Introduction," *Power and Landscape*, W. J. T. Mitchell (ed.), Chicago – London: Chicago University Press 1994, pp. 1–4, here p. 2.

teristic example of the earliest attempts to make symbolic representations seem natural by their "givenness as sight and site."

Republic Square is situated at the intersection of two central transport arteries: Bajseitov and Satpaev Avenues. 580 meters wide and 210 meters long, it was the official ceremonial square of Kazakhstan from 1972 until 1997. In 1972, a number of two-storied houses situated on the central north–south axis of the city were demolished in order to construct a modern square that was completed by 1980.[205] The square changed its name several times. Since 1980, its official title was Novaya (New). In 1982 it was renamed in honour of Leonid Brezhnev. In April 1988 the Council of Ministers decided to return to the initial name. Finally, in May 1990 the Supreme Council of the Kazakhstan adopted a resolution to rename Novaya as Republic Square.

After the acquisition of independence, state authorities decided to transform the design of the square. A complex including a stela, four sculptures, and reliefs with inscriptions eighteen meters high were built

Figure 4.1 Almaty: a view on Republic Square from the Main Entrance of the Almaty City Hall. Courtesy of Boris Chukhovich (private collection), 2017.

---

205 K. Nurmakov, N. Koyshybaev, A. Statenin, Yu. Tumanyan, A. Kapanov, K. Montakhayev, M. Pavlov, R. Seidalin were awarded the USSR State Prize for the design of the Square in 1982.

Figure 4.2 Monument of Independence of Kazakhstan in Almaty.
Source: Carwizard, Wikimedia Commons.

in its central part. The form of the stela is a symbolic reference to a *kulpy-tas*, a form of funeral statues, discovered on the territory of medieval Kazakhstan. The "Golden Man," standing on a snow leopard at the top of the stela, represents a warrior, created on the basis of an 1969 archeological excavation in the burial mound of Issyk, near Almaty, where a Scythian prince (or princess), vested in military equipment, was buried around 500 B.C.

Why a Scythian prince had to represent the Republic of Kazakhstan at the end of the twentieth century? Scythians lived on the present territory of Kazakhstan thousands of years ago. One possible interpretation is that the choice was made for the sake of instrumental appropriation: the tumulus was a major archeological discovery on the territory of contemporary Kazakhstan in the twentieth century. On the other hand, after the collapse of the USSR, and like many post-socialist countries, from Macedonia to Tajikistan, Kazakhstan was in a feverish search for powerful and representative ancestors. A monument representing Adam Mickiewicz, whom Belarus challenged Poland in claiming as a "national" poet, was erected in Minsk in 2003. An ambiguous warrior on horseback, suspiciously similar to Alexander the Great, appeared in Skopje in 2011. In Tashkent, Uzbekistan, the statue of Lenin on the main square was replaced by Tamerlane, to name but a few. In Central Asia, the only exception from this general trend was probably Turkmenistan, but only because all monuments and national celebrations were organized and dedicated to its leader, Saparmurat Nijazov, and his family. (After 2006, the monuments to Nijazov were gradually replaced by those dedicated to the new president, Gurbanguly Berdimuhamedow.)

Interestingly, many post-socialist states tried to excavate figures from the more distant past, since more recent figures were or could be contested by various groups of people. In the case of Kazakhstan, a number of representable statesmen were thought to be guilty of "collaborationism" with the Russian Empire[206] while others were not acceptable because they ruled only in one of three *Jüz*[207] and not in the other two. Thus, the Scythian prince provided a fascinating symbol that represented strength, greatness, and compromise at a moment when other historical figures were questionable.[208]

A group of four statues of a man ("A Sage"), a woman ("Mother-Earth"), and two equestrian statues of children are placed on the four sides around the stela. According to the authors of the monument,[209] the children signify youth and hope, and their parents, presumably, refer to a family. It also can be argued that the main elements of this representation, in particular the horses and clothing items, continue with the late-Soviet instrumentalisation of the Nomadic Myth, appropriated in order to give authenticity to a constructed "kazakhness." But what was nomadism in 1996 and what lay behind its appropriation at that time?

By the time when the monument was created, nomadism had long been eradicated. At the end of the 1920s, collectivisation occurred in Kazakhstan: the nomads' livestock was expropriated, and they were brought to so-called "sedentarisation points" under escort. By 1933, there

---

206 Amanzhol Kuzembayuly – Yerkin Abil', *Istoriya Kazakhstana*, Astana 2001, pp.158–167.

207 The meaning and origins of the jüz formations have been subject to different interpretations. Some researchers argued that originally jüz corresponded to tribal, military alliances of steppe nomads that emerged around the mid-sixteenth century after the disintegration of the Kazakh Khanate. Others proposed that jüz are geographical ecological zones separated by natural boundaries. Nomads adapted to these geographical zones and developed nomadic migration routes within the natural boundaries.

208 Irina V. Yerofeeva, "Sobytiia i liudi kazakhskoi stepi (epokha pozdnego srednevek'ia i novogo vremeni)," *Nauchnoe znanie i mifotvorchestvo v sovremennoi istoriografii Kazakhstana*, Zhulduzbek Abylkhozhin – Nurbulat Massanov – Irina Yerofeeva (eds.), Almaty: Daik-Press 2007, pp.132–224.

209 Shota Valihanov headed the project; Adilet Zhumabaev, Nurlan Dalban, and Kairat Suranchiev served as sculptors; Kazybek Zharilgapov served as architect. Architect Kaldybay Montahaev and sculptors Murat Mansurov, Azat Bayarlin, and Kazybek Satybaldin contributed to the project.

Figure 4.3 Republic Square, Almaty. Equestrian statues of children surrounding the stela. (Photo by Nari Shelekpayev, 2015)

remained only 1,727,000 sheep of more than twenty million in 1929.[210] As a result, one to two million people died of hunger between 1931 and 1933 and more than 40% of the native population left the country. The demographic outcome of this event was that ethnic Kazakhs only restored their pre-collectivisation population in 1970. The nomadic economy and way of life, with all its advantages and disadvantages, was lost forever.[211]

What happened to nomadism after collectivisation? Removed as a way of life, it kept its existence as a myth. According to Roland Barthes, "myth has the task of giving an historical intention a natural justification, and making contingency appear eternal. [...] The function of myth is to empty reality: it is, literally, a ceaseless flowing out, a haemorrhage, or perhaps an evaporation, in short a perceptible absence."[212] Numerous

---

210 Martha B. Olcott, "The Collectivization Drive in Kazakhstan," *The Russian Review* 40, no. 2 (1981), pp.123–136.

211 The approach to the interpretation of this tragedy changed considerably over time: from two lines in the Great Soviet Encyclopedia (GSE, Kazakhstan, 1969–1978) stating that "the result of collectivisation and industrialisation was the successful construction of a mainly socialist society," through cautious and weighted mentions of "collectivisation excesses" by Soviet historians in the 1960s and 1970s to a full recognition and a detailed description in monographs and post-Soviet text books.

212 Roland Barthes, *Mythologies*, New York: Farrar, Strauss and Giroux 1991, p. 142.

ideal representations of yurts, steppes, and nomads inhabited the pages of novels, the canvases of painters, theatre pieces, and opera performances in the middle and late-Soviet periods, blending very well with modernisation discourses and socialist realism.[213] All these representations were romanticized and devoid of any reference in time and space. Thus, post-nomadic society survived the tragedy, transforming it into a myth of the past, devoid of any dates, numbers or names.

Yet, if Soviet ideology developed the Nomadic Myth as an instrument of oblivion in order to subliminally form an idea of the antecedent of the nation, the 1996 State Commission, which accepted the new Republic Square project, presumably aimed to transform the already established passive myth into a more active instrument of ethnocentric nation-building. Four sculptures in Almaty were an early but not the only attempt to instrumentalise the nostalgia for nomadism.

A final element of the monument are ten horseshoe-shaped reliefs that depict, according to the authors of the composition, the most significant events in Kazakh history from ancient times until the present: the "Years of Great Disasters,"[214] the independence movement of the 1920s, the Zheltoksan, and the proclamation of independence[215] among others. It is important to note that several episodes from contemporary history, especially the 1986 Zheltoksan events were explicitly represented in an important public place for the first time.[216]

Many post-colonial ideologies used the struggle for independence as a powerful identity-construction symbol. For Kazakhstan this option was less evident, because the country obtained sovereignty not through revolution or anti-colonial struggle but through a relatively peaceful disintegration of the Soviet Union.[217] According to Edward Schatz, "unlike the Baltic republics and Ukraine, where the elites had managed to transform embryonic state apparatuses in the late 1980s by rallying them

---

213 In addition to music, painting, and landscape design appropriated earlier, cinema was also mobilized for nation-building purposes in the twenty-first century. See in particular Stephen M. Norris, "Nomadic Nationhood: Cinema, Nationhood, and Remembrance in Post-Soviet Kazakhstan," *Ab Imperio* 2 (2012), pp. 378–402.

214 Between 1720 and 1740 Kazakh lands were invaded by Jungars.

215 There are as well the inscriptions behind the Stela where the dates of the state sovereignty proclamation and the key states that recognized it are enumerated. There is also the president's palm print.

216 The December events in Almaty, also known as Zheltoksan, were spontaneous protests by Kazakh youth that took place in Almaty in December 1986 against the decision of the Central Political Bureau of the CP to dismiss from office the Secretary General of Kazakhstan D. Kunaev and replace him with G. Kolbin, a senior CP official who never worked in Kazakhstan before.

217 Cummings 2006, p. 177.

to the cause of ethnic nationalism, in Central Asia the independence movements were weak."[218] Rawi Abdelal noted that Kazakhstan was one of the post-Soviet countries that thoroughly marginalised its nationalist movements.[219] All this resulted in the fact that in 1990, 94% of the population voted for preserving the Soviet Union.[220] Indeed, if the Baltic states perceived membership in the Soviet Union as a burden, for Central Asian ones, especially after the Second World War, the situation was more ambiguous. In the second half of the twentieth century, the integration of the territories previously annexed by the Russian Empire in Central Asia by no means ground to a halt but instead accelerated. The Soviet government invested in the industrial, social, and cultural infrastructure in Kazakhstan, Uzbekistan, Kyrgyzstan, Turkmenistan, and Tajikistan. After the collapse of the Soviet Union and the disintegration of the common economy, post-Soviet Central Asian states faced de-industrialisation, political and social instability, and setbacks. Therefore, although the acquisition of independence was inscribed in the Almaty landscape by 1996, it was not entirely clear what kind of collective memory it was supposed to boost or reinforce.

In addition to the symbolic core, which represents a transformed image of the country, and a layer of reliefs representing a "historical" past, the square also accommodates the former government headquarters and other Brezhnev era buildings. These buildings are integrated into the square and serve as a broader frame to the stela, sculptures, and reliefs. Moreover, the square offers a beautiful view of the mountains surrounding the city.

Republic Square is thus a place where the material and symbolic layers melt in a complex spatial relationship that mirrors several overlapping temporalities. Its landscape, location, and history make this square unique: lying over the former Brezhnev Square, it is surrounded by a double frame of the Soviet era buildings and beautiful mountains. Almaty was the first city in Kazakhstan to experience a landscape transformation inspired by a political one. This transformation could only be partial because by 1991 Almaty had already been built up as a capital city and therefore lacked vacant space for the expression of a new image of the nation. However, twenty years later the example of an early

---

218 Schatz 2004, p. 124.

219 Rawi Abdelal, "Memories of Nations and States: Institutional History and National Identity in Post-Soviet Eurasia," *Nationalities Papers* 30, no. 3 (2002), pp. 459–460.

220 Valery A. Tishkov, *Ethnicity, Nationalism and Conflict in and after the Soviet Union: The Mind Aflame*, London: Sage 1997, p. 51.

post-Soviet redesign of its Republic Square enables us to grasp how the state wished to represent its new national identity before relocation of the capital city to Astana.

Astana: the Appropriation of the Future

The capital of Kazakhstan had officially moved from Almaty to Astana in 1997. Since that time the cityscape of the northern capital has experienced major transformations.[221] However, before discussing the image of Astana, it must first be explained why this undeveloped provincial town was chosen as capital city. In 1994, when the government decided to relocate the capital, the country's economy had been lagging and a common fear was that the costs related to the move would create an additional burden for the state budget. In a speech, pronounced on June 9, 1994 before the Supreme Council in Almaty, Kazakhstan's president Nursultan Nazarbayev said:

> "First, the capital must express the center of the state. It should not be close to someone or far from someone. It must be as far as possible from the borders. Another important factor: one square meter in Almaty costs 10–12 times more than in the center of Kazakhstan, because of seismic stability and so on. There is no place for the expansion of *this* city [emphasis added]. Its ecology does not stand up to any criticism. There are many examples in the world. In fact, there were two capitals in Russia – Leningrad, as we used to call it, and Moscow, Turkey has two capitals – Ankara and Istanbul, Pakistan has two capitals – Karachi and Islamabad, in Australia there are two capitals, Brazil has also relocated its capital city. There will be two cities in Kazakhstan. In the end, even for purely mercantile, practical purposes, it is cheaper and closer today to fly there. One last thing. An any case, we need to build a normal parliament building of this state – with a residential complex, with offices for employees, for all in one place, with all amenities. We still need to build the Presidential House, a normal Governmental House, not the one designed for the Central Committee [of the Communist Party]. Where are we going to do this?"[222]

---

221 "Northern capital" is one way to call Astana in Kazakhstan. The "Southern capital" is Almaty.

222 National Archives of Kazakhstan, f. 2, op. 4, d.257, l. 35. Minutes of the First Session of the 13th Supreme Council of the Republic of Kazakhstan.

As one can see, the president appealed to the fact that the former capital was situated in a zone of high seismic activity, had major ecological problems, was too close to the southern borders and lacked free space for building the governmental offices. The president also mentioned the examples of other capital cities' relocation across the globe in order to reinforce his argument. On the other hand, unofficial discourses invoked the danger of separatism from the northern and north-western regions of the country and interpreted the relocation project as a desire to reinforce political control with the help of geopolitical means.[223] At the end, Astana was chosen because it was conveniently connected to other parts of Kazakhstan by rail, and also because it had a potential for economic and infrastructural growth, and no major ecological problems. The image of the city, however, needed to be transformed: the new capital did not have a recognizable urban identity.

Astana boasts a spacious steppe landscape; it is situated in the transitional area between the fertile northern lands of Kazakhstan full of forests and the dry, poor territories in the centre. The older parts of the city lie to the north of the Ishim river, which constitutes a border between them and the new quarters, located on the southern side.

Figure 4.4 View of Tselinograd (Astana), 1976. Municipal Archives of Astana. Private collection of Andrej Dubitskij.

223 Schatz 2004, p. 124.

Unlike Almaty's Republic Square, transformed on the basis of the existing place, the governmental district in Astana was designed and built from scratch.

Astana was inaugurated in 1998 but it was a few years later that the government decided to re-conceptualize the cityscape by extending its territory to the southern part of the city, located at the left bank of Ishim. This decision became a turning point in the life of Astana: earlier interventions were mainly attempts to transform the existing landscape, while going to the other side of the river meant a physical and symbolic detachment from the previous spatial schemes and their limits. The Japanese architect Kisho Kurokawa and his collaborators designed a new general plan of Astana. His intention was that the plan be reviewed every five years and, if necessary, modified in a flexible way. "Traditional master plans have always given great importance to the process of finalizing the ideal form. In contrast with the traditional idea of these master plans, Kurokawa's proposal (Master System) treats the question of what would be the city of the 21st century."[224]

The public space created on the left bank was spacious and brand-new. Presidential, parliamentary, and governmental complexes; ministries and the Supreme Court; National Library and Archives; several major trade and entertainment complexes and the Palace of Peace and Reconciliation are laid out along a single axis.[225] The central element of this axis is *Bayterek*[226] – the Independence Monument. The ninety-seven meter high tower, made of metal, glass, and concrete, symbolises the year 1997 when the capital city was relocated. Its sphere is twenty-two meters in diameter and weighs 300 tons, supported by a 1000-ton metal body standing on solid pylons. According to the official sources, including the information provided for the tourists in situ, the legend behind the structure supposedly comes from "ancient Turkic mythology."[227] The appropriation of the left bank did not end with the a few important buildings along the axis: a variety of structures were or are being erected in the southwestern part of the city.

According to Edward Schatz, "state building should not be conceptually reduced to the development and location of bureaucratic apparatus.

224 Kisho Kurokawa, *Works and Projects, Master Plan for the New Capital of Kazakhstan*, Astana 1997.
225 All of the buildings were created between 2003 and 2011. Khan-Shatyr and the Palace of Peace and Reconciliation were created by Foster & Partners.
226 Meaning "poplar tree" in Kazakh.
227 The only written source of this legend that I was able to collect is a short story, *Er-Targyn*, published in the collection of Kazakh fairy-tales in the 1980s.

Figure 4.5 Astana - Bayterek.
Source: Sergej Marcynjuk, Wikimedia Commons.

It involves constructing a symbolic order to propagate ideas about an elite's political legitimacy, cultural rectitude, and effectiveness in governance. It involves setting the terms of a normative regime."[228] If an urban plan is considered not as a merely functional document but as part of an effort to construct "a symbolic order," the Astana city plan undoubtedly represents a breakthrough in contemporary Kazakhstan's urban planning both in aesthetic and ideological terms. Kisho Kurokawa's proposal, supported by the state authorities, consisted in creating a "symbiosis" of a new city adjacent to the old one. The master plan, elaborated under his guidance, contrasted with previous approaches to the planning of Tselinograd and Akmola.[229] According to Kurokawa's proposal, planners and municipal authorities should "aim at the future" and "create a sustainable city of the 21st century."[230] Given the economic conditions

228 Schatz 2004, p. 120.
229 Previous names of Astana.
230 Kisho Kurokawa,"International Competition for the Master Plan and Design of Astana, Kazakhstan." Works and Projects, Accessible at: http://www.kisho.co.jp/page.php/222. Last retrieved 15 March 2013.

of 1998, this was, without any doubt, a utopian project. Accordingly, documents of a propagandist nature declare Astana a "new" city, and its foundation date the year 1998.[231]

Even though the newly built governmental district on the left bank is physically smaller than older parts of the city lying on the right bank, it is important at psychological and symbolic levels. When Astana is shown on television, it is the left bank that generally appears on the screen. Through postcards, albums, and recently published books, Astana is represented as a modern city, a cloudless *Civitas Solis*, "aiming at the future," with its colonial and Soviet past hidden on the right bank where most people live. The new city is detached from the old one by the river which serves as a barrier between the two. As for the "old" city, no wholesale destruction of Soviet epoch buildings occurred there: most of them are being maintained until sufficient new housing can be provided. However, as more and more people who need accommodation are migrating to Astana, the circle closes. "Freshmen" buy or rent apartments in old buildings, while a new bourgeoisie moves from to the left bank. Moving to the south means crossing a social Rubicon: since it was primarily conceived as an administrative area, the cost of real estate is very high. Consequently, only few can afford both to work and to live on the left bank. Thousands of young clerks commute daily by car from the right side where they live to the left side where they work (often through carpooling or taking a common taxi) or by public transport.

Thus, a post-Soviet design of the left bank is not only an ideological appropriation of space, or a "claim to territorialisation," as it was for the square in Almaty, but an embodied detachment from the past, a transformation of space into an active instrument of nation-building and a showcase for the international community. If one compares Almaty and Astana, the former transformed its existing material space in order to fill it with a new symbolic content while the latter created the space anew in order to signify, not only by its materiality but also by the very fact of its creation, a desire for a new symbolic order.

However, grasping the role played by Astana in relation to the nation-building of contemporary Kazakhstan does not mean that its material and social construction should be taken for granted. On the contrary, its further problematisation is necessary since Astana is hardly the result of standard urban development projects or the product of market-driv-

---

231 See for instance, the Astana Expo 2017 promotion materials in English and in French. Accessible at: https://expo2017astana.com/en/. Last retrieved 15 July 2016.

en forces. Rather, it is the fruit of a single person's (or a small group of persons') vision as well as a further effort by that group to legitimise this vision. Kazakhstan's president Nursultan Nazarbayev dominates the discourse on the construction of Astana as "planner" and "creator". A handful of renowned architects such as Kisho Kurokawa, Norman Foster, and Manfredi Nicoletti share this role with the former as they created projects for Astana, either by direct invitation by the authorities or through winning open competitions. However, not only architects participated in the legitimation of the new capital city. Italian singer Andrea Bocelli performed during the opening ceremony of Khan-Shatyr, a fashionable shopping mall designed by Norman Foster. Montserrat Caballé was invited to the opening ceremony of the Pyramid of Peace and Reconciliation, also designed by Foster. *Cirque du Soleil* performed at the Astana City anniversary in 2012. However, architects presumably played a more significant role due to the visibility and durability of their efforts.

Conclusion

Since 1997, the attitudes of people regarding Astana have considerably improved, from a negation at the end of the 1990s to enthusiasm in the 2000s.

The nation is an imagined community in the sense that it can never be lived or perceived by its members within their direct experience and only imagination can help to recreate a supposed integrity with its other representatives.[232] Does Astana's left bank make Kazakhstan's people a more united community? Apparently, it does, but only until the moment when people can really live the dichotomy of the left and the right banks. The left bank is the centre of the government, physically detached from the right bank where most people live. The left bank restaurants, entertainment centres, and malls are too expensive for the average income of the people. As a result, the real experience of the left bank is a detachment: physical, and social. Directed outwards, it is an illusory representation of the nation rather than a process aiming at national unity.

Nation-building is a never-ending process. New actors, political shifts, as well as technological and economic transformations may provoke an adjustment of the existing representations. The period between

---

232 Benedict Anderson, *Imagined Communities: Reflections on the Origin and Spread of Nationalism*, London – New York: Verso 2006, pp. 1–30, 74–76, 100–116.

1991 and 2001 was particularly intense in the history of Kazakhstan's nation-building. Although it resembled other post-Soviet countries, it also had a number of distinct features. Due to the heterogeneity of ethnic and linguistic situation, strong regionalisms, and a gap between urban and rural populations, the government could not adopt language and education extensively as nation-building tools, although the attempts to do so were not totally unsuccessful. In the mid-1990s, the government made a radical step and relocated the capital city to the north. In 1998, Kazakhstan became the only country in the former USSR and the last country in the 20th century to change its governmental site. Unlike Almaty, where any spatial transformations could only be partial because of its previous role, Astana had vacant territories on the left bank of Ishim where the state could build from scratch. The symbolic and material construction of these territories gradually came to symbolize the new identity of the post-Soviet Kazakhstan.

Is Name Destiny? On Some Cases of Post-Soviet Street-Naming in Almaty and Astana

Nari Shelekpayev

"Generally speaking, it was the African countries like Zaire, Benin, Burkina Faso, Côte d'Ivoire and to a lesser extent – Asian countries – which, in order to make political pressure, decided to change their names. The attempt of the Burmese leadership to dictate the naming of the country according to the autochthonous phonetics (Myanmar) produced a backlash from the rest of the world. Our own experience has demonstrated how ambiguous the attitude of the international community was towards the attempt to adapt the name of our capital city in accordance with Kazakh traditions."

From a memo by the Minister of Foreign Affairs K. Saudabayev addressed to the President of Kazakhstan Nursultan Nazarbayev on August 2, 1994.[233]

Introduction

In February 2014, Nursultan Nazarbayev, the unchallenged leader of Kazakhstan since 1989, proposed to change the official name of his country to Kazakh Yeli (Kazakh State). Although the proposal was widely reported and created an important public debate, the ultimate decision regarding renaming was suspended.[234] In 2015, on the eve of the Kazakh Khanate's 550th anniversary celebration, the municipal administration of Almaty – former capital and largest city in Kazakhstan – announced that "at least ten streets in the city would bear former Kazakh khans' names in

---

233 Presidential Archives of the Republic of Kazakhstan, Almaty, 5H, 1, 3387 (my translation from Russian).

234 "Nazarbayev vydvinul ideju pereimenovat' Kazahstan." Accessible at: http://www.forbes.ru/, 6 February 2014. Last retrieved 15 August 2014.

the near future."[235] These recent developments hint that after 25 years of sovereignty, Kazakhstan's quest for its "national idea" is on full blast and that place-naming mirrors this process. Despite being perceived by many as leading to an eventual rupture, the process of place-renaming is supposed to create a symbolic extension towards a longer "national" past.

Street-Naming and National Identity

The Soviet Union began to disintegrate in the late 1980s following unsuccessful reforms, unfavorable economic conditions, and the rise of democratic movements inside the Union. By the end of 1991, fifteen states of the former Soviet Union had declared their independence. Each republic had a unique experience stemming from variations in historical and political factors. However, all would utilize democratic and nationalistic rhetoric when differentiating new regimes from the past. The term "transition" became a cliché meaning post-communist in politics, neo-liberal in economy, and something ambiguous in other spheres. Gradually, the initial meaning of transition as a movement towards a new beginning was replaced by a perception of it as the new permanent. No one knew how long the transition was to last and when exactly it would end. One of the more remarkable features of this period was the adoption of a new visual language that post-Soviet states invented to aid the distinction from the previous political regime. Kazakhstan adopted its own currency, with Al-Farabi portraits printed on, and reinforced the status of the Kazakh language. The names of many cities, streets, and squares changed as part of the linguistic and cultural appropriation of the Soviet street-naming by the independent Kazakhstan. This chapter intends to examine several cases of street-renaming in Almaty and Astana in the 1990s and describe its main features.

To date, some research has been done concerning the construction of national identity in the post-Soviet Kazakhstan.[236] Recent works mainly

---

235 "V Almaty planirujut pomenjat' nazvanija desjati uliz," *Kazakhstanskaya pravda*, 22 June 2015. Accessible at: http://www.kazpravda.kz/news/obshchestvo/v-almati-planiruut-pomenyat-nazvaniya-desyati-ulits/. Last retrieved 22 January 2016.

236 See Ravi Abdelal, "Memories of Nations and States: Institutional History and National Identity in Post-Soviet Eurasia," *Nationalities Papers* 30, no. 3 (2002), pp. 459–460; Alexander C. Diener, "National Territory and the Reconstruction of History in Kazakhstan," *Eurasian Geography and Economics* 43, no. 8 (2002), pp. 632–650; Edward Schatz, "What Capital Cities Say about State and Nation Building," *Nationalism and Ethnic Politics* 9, no. 4 (2004), pp. 111–140; Sally N. Cummings, "Legitimation and Identification in Kazakhstan," *Nationalism and Ethnic Politics*

emphasise the political aspects of this construction and its main protago-nists, while its impact on place-naming in the key cities has been less ex-plored. As for toponymy, this field is situated at the crossroads of urban history, sociology, cultural geography, and nationalism studies.[237] To my knowledge, there exists almost no research that applies recent develop-ments from this field to post-Soviet Kazakhstan.[238] This chapter does not pretend to mention and even less to analyze all important transforma-tions in Kazakhstan's place-naming since 1991, neither does it propose to develop a theoretical argument concerning the field of place-naming studies. Instead, it aims to perform a limited analysis of several cases in two major Kazakh cities with a particular focus on place-naming as a practice of (a) legitimation, (b) commemoration, and (c) naturalisation of the political order in post-Soviet Kazakhstan. Pierre Bourdieu pointed out that:

"the almost magical power of words comes from the fact that the objectifi-cation and de facto officialisation brought about by the public act of nam-ing, in front of everyone, has the effect of freeing the particularity (which lies at the source of all sense of identity) from the unthought, and even unthinkable. [...] And officialisation finds its fulfilment in demonstration, the typically magical (which does not mean ineffectual) act through which the practical group – virtual, ignored, denied, or repressed – makes it-self visible and manifest, for other groups and for itself, and attests to its existence as a group that is known and recognised, laying a claim to institutionalisation."[239]

12, no. 2 (2006), pp. 177–204; Donnacha O. Beacháin – Rob Kevlihan, "Threading the Needle: Kazakhstan between Civic and Ethno-Nationalistic State-Building," *Nations and Nationalism* 19, no. 2 (2013), pp. 337–356.

237 See Kari Palonen, "Reading Street Names Politically," *Reading the Political: Exploring the Margins of Politics*, Kari Palonen – Tuija Parvikko (eds.), Tampere: Finnish Political Science Association 1993, pp. 103–121; Maoz Azaryahu, "The Power of Commemorative Street Names," *Environment and Planning D: Society and Space* 14, no. 3 (1996), pp. 311–330; Frank R. Hamlin, "Numbers in Placenames," *Names: A Journal of Onomastics* 47, no. 3 (1999), pp. 233–242; Stuart Elden, "Governmentality, Calculation, Territory," *Environment and Planning D: Society and Space* 25, no. 3 (2007), pp. 562–580; Derek Alderman, "Place, Naming, and the Interpretation of Cultural Landscapes," *The Ashgate Research Companion to Heritage and Identity*, Brian Graham – Peter Howard (eds.), Burlington: Ashgate 2008, pp. 195–213; Reuben Rose-Redwood – Derek Alderman – Maoz Azaryahu, "Geographies of Toponymic Inscription: New Directions in Critical Place-Name Studies," *Progress in Human Geography* 34, no. 4 (2010), pp. 453–470.

238 The text was written in 2013 and could not consider the subsequent changes.

239 Pierre Bourdieu, *Language and Symbolic Power*, John B. Thompson (ed.), English trans. by G. Raymond and M. Adamson, Cambridge: Polity Press 1991, p. 224.

In Bourdieu's view, (re-)naming is driven by an intention which he depicts as "magical." "Magic" may imply a theatricality, inherent to the act of re-naming and which the effectiveness is ensured by the presence of an audience, to which it is directed as a symbolic act. The word "magical" does not necessarily mean that re/naming has only a symbolic value; for magic can be backed up by an intention to transform the symbolic capital, achieved through the act of re-naming, into the economic or political one. Also, Bourdieu draws attention to the fact that the act of re-commemoration is also a shift in the position of dominated and dominant – where the "virtual, ignored, denied, or repressed" seek to fix the changed attitudes to them as a social group. In other words, what is important is not only the idiosyncrasy of a newly introduced name regardless of its possible connotation, and not the naming system as a whole, but the very act of renaming, that serves as a tool of demonstration or affirmation for a given group.

Another important facet of renaming is related to the idea of commemoration. According to Pierre Nora,

> "Lieux de mémoires are simple and ambiguous, natural and artificial, at once immediately available in concrete sensual experience and susceptible to the most abstract elaboration. Indeed, they are lieux in three senses of the word – material, symbolic, and functional."[240]

More recently, in an article that synthesizes and interrogates some recent developments in the field of critical place-naming studies, Reuben Rose-Redwood argued that renaming as a commemorative practice is in fact an active instrument that promotes and naturalizes a certain ideology:

> "The version of history that commemorative place naming introduces into social communication is experienced as obvious, part of the 'natural order.' In this sense, the apparent weakness of the historical reference actually augments the power of commemorative place names to render a certain version of history not only familiar, but also self-evident. The merit of a place name as a commemorative vehicle is that it transforms an official discourse of history into a shared cultural experience that is embedded into practices of everyday life."[241]

---

240 Pierre Nora, "Between Memory and History: les lieux de memoirs," *Representations* 26 (1989), p. 7.
241 Rose-Redwood – Alderman – Azaryahu 2010, p. 459.

While Bourdieu theorized what the re-naming represented for those who implement it (i.e., the state acting on behalf of its agents), Rose-Redwood suggested to include the impact of re-naming on those who experience it in order to understand how the "banalisation" of a changed order of things (or a transformation of bourdieusian "magic" into a routine) occurs. The approach to re-naming as a tool which transforms the surrounding reality in order to better control or manage it informs the analysis of several cases of street-renaming in Almaty and Astana which will be developed in this chapter.

The Case of Almaty

Back in 1989, a massive renaming of streets and squares and a sweeping out of communist names was unthinkable. Yet, since 1991 "a magical act of demonstration" gradually spread throughout the entire country.[242] According to information from the Almaty Inquiry Service, between 1991 and 2001, approximately 170 streets were renamed. Given the total of 833 streets that existed in Almaty in 2011, this is not a big number.[243] However, streets differ in size and importance: the (non)renaming of an avenue located in the city center, and a side street on the periphery have different implications. Also, a renaming, if important and visible, is not an absolute indicator of a major identity change. Minsk, for instance, had an important renaming campaign in the 1990s, but even today it bears very strong features of Soviet identity. Another controversial example is the capital of Turkmenistan, Ashgabat, where squares and monuments in honor of Saparmurat Niyazov have gradually been replaced by a glorification of Gurbanguly Berdimuhamedow after the 2006 political shift.[244]

---

242 In fact, the name of the country changed as well. During the first years of the Soviet Union, Kazakhstan was called the Kyrgyz Autonomous Socialist Republic within the Russian Soviet Federal Socialist Republic. In 1925, it became the Kazakh Autonomous Soviet Socialist Republic and in 1936, the Kazakh Soviet Socialist Republic of the Union of Soviet Socialist Republics. Finally, in 1991 the Republic of Kazakhstan became the official name of the country.
243 Data from a report of Onomasticheskaja Komissija pri Akimate goroda Almaty [Municipal Onomastics Commission of the Municipal Government of the City of Almaty], 2010.
244 Saparmurat Niyazov (Turkmenbashi) was the leader of Turkmenistan from 1985 until his death in 2006. Gurbanguly Berdymuhammedov (Arkadag) has been Turkmenistan's president since 2006.

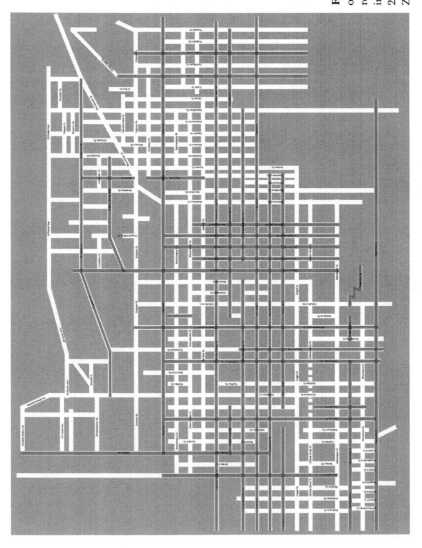

Figure 5.1 The map of Almaty with largest renamed streets marked in grey; state by the year 2001. (Created by Zarina Zhimailova)

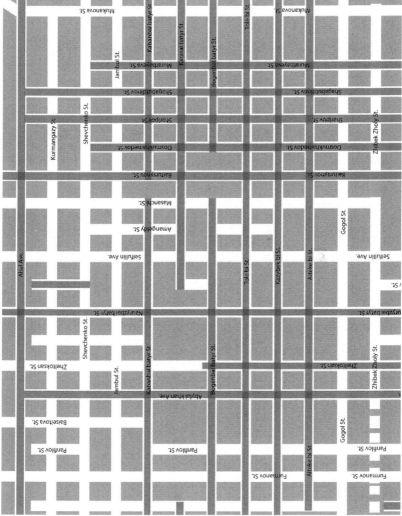

Figure 5.2 A detail of the map of Almaty with the largest renamed streets marked in grey; state by the year 2001. (Created by Zarina Zhimailova)

Maoz Azaryahu mentioned three renaming strategies in a postcolonial[245] context: "One is to erase all 'colonial' street names as well as pulling down 'colonial' monuments to signify a complete break from colonial past. [...] The other extreme is to leave colonial commemorations in their place. [...] A third strategy is a selective de-commemoration of the colonial past."[246] Post-Soviet place-naming in Almaty adopts a mix of the second and third strategies.

The foundation of contemporary Almaty dates back to 1854, when the imperial government decided to build a fortification called *Zailijskoe* on the left bank of the river *Malaya Almatinka*. This fortification was renamed Verniy after a year. Later the city twice changed its name. The Brockhaus and Efron Encyclopedic Dictionary (1890–1916) dedicated a separate chapter to the city. It states that

> "[...] a new fortification of Vernyi was founded on the place of the former settlement of Alma-Aty (Apple Valley), to protect the latter from the raids of the savage Kara-Kyrgyz. So, Vernyi fortification was the first administrative center of the Alatavskij district of the Semipalatinskij Region. Later, the formation of the Turkestan Military District and the Semirechenskij Region led to the establishment of the administrative centre for the region here under the name of Verniy. Natives and Russians, however, kept calling it Alma-Aty."[247]

This passage hints at a double naming of the city which mirrored its multifaceted identity. In 1921, after the October Revolution, Vernyi

---

245 Generally speaking, if the term "postcolonial" implies both a historical periodization and a mode of analysis or critique, "post-soviet" is, at present, mainly a descriptive term meaning "after 1989" or "located in the former USSR." The difficulties of lumping the "soviet" into the "colonial"(and "post-Soviet" into 'postcolonial') range from a general lack of conceptualizations of the Soviet Union as an object of colonial study, to the Soviet Union's ambiguous "coloniality," to which may be added the presumably unachieved postcolonial condition of Kazakhstan and other post-Soviet Central Asian states and so on. For details see: Laura Adams, "Can We Apply Postcolonial Theory to Central Eurasia?", *Central Eurasian Studies Review* 7, no. 1 (2008), pp. 2–7; Gayatri Chakravorty Spivak – Nancy Condee – Harsha Ram – Vitaly Chernetsky, "Are We Postcolonial? Post-Soviet Space," *Publications of the Modern Languages Association* 121, no. 3 (2006), pp. 819–836; David Chioni Moore, "Is the Post in Postcolonial the Post in Post-Soviet? Notes toward a Global Postcolonial Critique," *Publications of the Modern Languages Association* 116, no. 1 (2001), pp. 111–128.
246 Maoz Azaryahu, "The Critical Turn and Beyond: The Case of Commemorative Street Naming," *ACME: An International E-Journal for Critical Geographies* 10, no. 1 (2011), pp. 28–33.
247 The Brockhaus and Efron Encyclopedic Dictionary (86 volumes), article: Verniy, Saint-Petersbourg, 1890–1907. (Translation from Russian by the author of this chapter).

Figure 5.3 A list of selected former and current street names in Almaty. (Created by Nari Shelekpayev).

Current name	Former name
Ablai Khan	Kommunisticheskij
Aiteke Bi	Oktjabr'skij
Aldar Kose	Zenkov
Altynsarin	Pravda
Bajkadamov	Kihtenko
Bekmahanov	Sovetskaja Konstitucija
Bogenbaj Batyr	Kirov
Buhar Zhyrau	Botanicheskij
Dostyk	Lenin
Zheltoksan	Mir
Zhibek Zholy	Gorkij
Kabanbaj Batyr	Kalinin
Kazybek Bi	Sovetskij
Kasteev	Podgornaja
Kunaev	Karl Marx
Majlin	Kremlevskij
Moldagulova	Slobodskaja
Prokof'ev	Ushakov
Xi Xinhai	Vladimirskij
Tole Bi	Komsomolskij
Turgut Özal	Bauman
Fizuli	23 parts"ezd
Shakarim	Zhdanov
Yassawi	Centralnij

was renamed *Alma-Ata*. (The old name irritated the Bolsheviks: Vernyj literally meant "loyal" to the tsar which it was. In 1993, Alma-Ata was renamed *Almaty*, to reflect more properly the grammar and stylistics of the Kazakh language.

In the past, many street names reflected various stages of spatial and temporal advancement of the Soviet regime through both direct and indirect references: Kazakhstan Komsomol's 10th Anniversary, 23rd Party Congress, 50 years of October Revolution, Communist, Lenin, Red

Partisans, Soviet, and so on.[248] Some names pointed to the industrial
features of the city: Brick, Industrial, Railway are a few examples. Many
streets bore names of the revolution and war heroes, such as Chapaev,
Frunze, Dzerzhinskij; or eminent scientists and scholars, such as Sofiya
Kovalevskaja, Louis Pasteur, Ivan Michurin, or Nikolai Lobachevskij.
A few names referred to various places, important from historical or military points of view, such as Danube, Leningrad, Port Arthur, or Warsaw.
Finally, a number of street names pointed to the local history and the
characteristics of the city founders, such as Pear, Rose, Cossack, or Zen-
kov – a former city planner.[249]

After 1991, a new political conjuncture called into question many
previous names. The process was double-edged: in some instances, the
reminders of the Soviet past have been deleted from the urban text for
good. In others, the deleted inscriptions were replaced by new ones,
reflecting the identity of a more "Kazakh" Kazakhstan. Consequently,
many streets were renamed in honor of notable personalities, places,
historical events, etc. The updated street-naming had an explicit connection with pre-Soviet Kazakhstan and with some ethnic Kazakhs from
the Soviet Union. Specifically, Almaty's central avenues were renamed
in honor of Kazybek bi, Nauryzbaj Batyr, Ablaj Khan and so on. Other
streets were renamed in honor of musicians such as Shamshi Kaldaja-
kov, Gaziza Zhubanova, poets and aqyns Akan-Sery, Mukagali Maka-
taev, Anuar Alimzhanov. Many of these people either lived or worked
in Almaty. In some cases special plaques, explaining the biography of
the commemorated persons, were introduced. Some names referred to
the historical geography of Kazakhstan: for example Turkestan (former
Machine-builders') and Otrar (former Igor Kurchatov). Interestingly,
Brezhnev Square was renamed into Republic Square.

However, it would be overly simplified to claim that previous "Soviet"
toponyms were simply erased and replaced by "Kazakh" ones. The situation was more complex, not only due to the "Soviet" origin of many newly commemorated personalities but also parts of new names were related
to neither "old" nor "new" epochs. For instance, Nikolay Bauman street
was renamed in honour of Turgut Özal.[250] Turgut Özal was President
of Turkey from 1989 to 1993. Turkey was the first country to officially

248 In this part of the text only a few cases of re-naming will be analyzed. It is possible that some
   of the cases mentioned here have already been renamed or ceased to exist.
249 *Gruchevij* means "Pear," *Kazachij* – "Cossack," *Rozovij* – "Rose." Zenkov was the chief architect
   for Almaty at the end of the nineteenth century.
250 Nikolai Bauman (1873–1905) was a professional Russian revolutionary of the Bolshevik party.

recognize Kazakhstan as an independent state, immediately after it proclaimed sovereignty. Also, Turkish investments in Kazakhstan's economy were considerable in the 1990s. In addition, during the 1990s Turkey initiated the opening of twenty-four Kazakh-Turkish schools, Kazakh-Turkish Khoja Ahmed Yassawi University in Turkestan, as well as Suleiman Demirel University in Almaty. All of these institutions became providers of the Turkish language and, according to some accounts, pan-Turkic ideology in Kazakhstan.

In fact, the 1990s were a period of an intense search for a suitable geopolitical strategy for Kazakhstan. In the 1990s, Kazakhstan actively cooperated with Turkey, considering its model of secular conservatism an inspiring example for its own nation-building. Turkey was described in the speeches of politicians and the media as a "culturally close" example of successful economic and political modernization, thirsted for by Kazakhstan in the 1990s. Turkey, for its part, has been very supportive and active in Central Asia, hoping to increase its influence and become a privileged partner for a new region of Central Asia, in stark contrast to Russia. However, since the beginning of the 2000s Turkey has been gradually losing its political importance for Kazakhstan. The two countries still cooperate on many issues, and a number of bilateral visits on various levels occur each year, yet the state of Kazakh-Turkish bilateral relations is far from the hedonism of the 1990s. Nevertheless, no other central street in Almaty received the name of a foreign politician except the above-mentioned Turgut Özal. The situation is different in Astana: after the visit of French prime-minister François Fillon in 2008, the Ministry of Foreign Affairs pressed for the renaming of a street in honor of Charles de Gaulle. Other such examples would be the renaming of a street in Astana in honor of Geidar Aliev, former president of Azerbaijan, and another one in honor of King Hussein of Jordan.[251]

As for local politicians, one street in Almaty was renamed in honor of Dinmukhamed Kunaev, who ran the Communist Party of the Kazakhstan for more than twenty years, from 1964 to 1986. In 1986, accusations of corruption and cronyism led to Kunaev's resignation. Gennadij Kolbin, Kunaev's successor, was replaced by Nursultan Nazarbayev three years later. The commemoration of Kunaev in Almaty may be interpreted as a recognition of this politician's merits. Apart from Kunaev, other emblematic names that had long been suppressed or considered taboo, such as Ahmed Baytursynov, Zhusupbek Aymauytov, and Magzhan Zhum-

---

251 Other recent examples are not covered by this study.

abaev, which were wiped out during the Stalinist Terror in the 1930s, reappeared in Almaty.

Domostroitelnij (House-building) was renamed in honour of Ulugbek, Bezimyannij (Nameless) in honour of Dulati, and XXIII S'ezd Partii in honor of Fuzûlî. The astronomer Ulugbek lived in Samarkand, while the historian Dulati was born in Tashkent and died in Kashmir in the 16th century. The poet and philosopher Fuzûlî lived in the Ottoman Empire and is considered Azeri in Azerbaijan, and a Turk in Turkey. The three above-mentioned cases are a statement that Kazakhstan aspires to represent itself as entitled to the spiritual and scientific heritage of the greater Central Asian civilization.

On the contrary, Yevgenij Brusilovskij and Sergei Prokofiev (which replaced little unknown Rudnev and Ushakov) lived in Kazakhstan and were connected to Almaty professionally: for instance, Brusilovskij spent many years in Almaty and contributed to the professionalization of classical music in Kazakhstan. He composed several operas, symphonies, ballets, and other works. Prokofiev arrived in Almaty in 1943 to join the evacuated Sergei Eisenstein to compose film music for *Ivan the Terrible*, and the ballet *Cinderella*. In both cases, the renaming was intended as a reminder of the role and the importance of non-natives who worked in Kazakhstan and contributed to the development of its culture and construction of the artistic *milieu* of Almaty.

The commemoration of Manas (former Chapaev) and Aldar Kose (former Zenkov) stand out from the general picture. Aldar Kose is not a real person but a hero from tales and anecdotes, an invented "man of the people", who by deceiving the wealthy, gained their money and valuables. The literature on Aldar Kose provides an example of the invention of a "vernacular" character by the Soviet folklorists. After 1991 Aldar was not forgotten. In 2005, this character was represented on stamps (with a face value of 30, 35, and 40 tenghe).[252] As for Manas, the commemoration of this Kyrgyz epic may be seen as a tribute to the southern neighbor of Kazakhstan and its national identity.

Where are the above-mentioned streets situated? Almaty is crossed horizontally by the large Ryskulov, Raymbek, Tole Bi, Abay, Satpayev, Zhandosov, Timirjazev, and Al-Farabi avenues. Vertically, there are Auezov, Sain, Navoi, Rozybakiev, Zharokov, Seifullin, Nauryzbai-Batyr, Abylai Khan, and Dostyk. Six of these seventeen have been renamed: Tole bi (former Komsomolskij), Auezov (former Fifth Line), Navoy (for-

---

252 Tenghe is Kazakhstan's national currency.

mer Vishnevskij), Rozybakiev (former Seventeenth Line), Ablai Khan (former Kommunisticheskij), and Dostyk (former Lenin). Such transformations are evolutionary rather than revolutionary: one could hardly claim that the place-naming in Almaty completely lost its previous features. The contemporary street-naming of post-Soviet Almaty thus became a cocktail of colonial and Soviet sub-strata, which may be said to be gradually replaced by a "primordial" super-stratum, combining real and legendary names and references to a "Kazakh" Kazakhstan and the broader Central Asian region.

The Case of Astana

Initially a fortress on the river Ishim, what is today Kazakhstan's capital was founded by the Russian imperial administration in 1824. Later the fortress transformed itself into a small population aggregate, named Akmolinsk. During the early twentieth century, the town became an important railway junction, causing a major economic boom that lasted until 1917. In 1961, Akmolinsk was renamed Tselinograd (Virgin Lands City) and became the capital of the Virgin Lands Territory (Tselinnyj Kraj). Since the late 1950s large numbers of immigrants were constantly arriving to the Virgin Lands, with many of them eventually deciding to settle down in Kazakhstan. Following Kazakhstan's independence in 1991, the city was renamed Akmola, literally meaning "White Shrine" or "White Mausoleum." In 1997, the capital city was officially relocated from Almaty to Akmola. The new name, Astana, was bestowed in 1998. The word *Astana* in Kazakh literally means *capital*.

Fifty-eight streets changed their names in Astana between 1993 and 2003. It is important to mention that Astana has continually been under construction since 1997. Thus, many names emerge through the direct construction of streets and squares, rather than as a result of renaming.

The source of inspiration for the invention of new street names in Astana is was many ways similar to Almaty. Soviet names, such as Red Star, Socialist, Krupskaja, 50 years of October, Komsomol, Soviet Constitution, Red Army, October, Lenin, Mikoyan, gradually vanished along with industrial names such as Asphalt, Timber Mill, or Workers'. Interestingly, Tselinnik, referring to the Virgin Lands Campaign, disappeared altogether with Tselinograd – the former name of Astana. This became a *coup de grâce* for a previous identity of the city so strongly connected to the modernization of the 1960s.

Known and unknown Soviet revolutionaries and personalities (Budennyj, Ordzhonikidze, Lihachev, Drizge, Monin, Kalachev, Katchenko, Shvernik, Telmann, Avdeev); a few non-vernacular names of the Great Patriotic War heroes such as Kuibyshev and Grekov; and featureless identifications such as Vokzalnij (Railway Station), Polevoj (Field), or Dalnij (Remote) sank into oblivion. Yet the names on a selection of monuments remained intact.[253] Some names did disappear only to later resurface in a new location. For instance, former Abaj street was renamed in honour of Kubrin, however Abaj avenue was established later in a more prestigious place.

Astana commemorated some eighteenth and nineteenth century personalities, including Birzhan-sal, Kenesary, and Ablai Khan. Also, a belated tribute was paid to the Kazakh intelligentsia exterminated during the Stalinist purges in the 1930s: Alikhan Bukeyhan, Turar Ryskulov, Mukhamedzhan Tynyshbaev, and Myrzhakyp Dulatov, to name a few.

Astana also commemorated a number of artists and writers who worked in the second half of the 20th century, including Anuar Alimzhanov, Gabiden Mustafin, Ilyas Esenberlin, Nurgisa Tlendiev, Michail Zataevich and so on. A couple of renamed streets refer to the very recent past: for example, Zheltoksan and Ryskulbekov directly point to the events of December 1986 when Kazakh youth organized an anti-governmental riot. Some names were translated from Russian into Kazakh or changed to a more authentic spelling: Mir became Bejbitshilik and Valikhanov – Ualihanov.[254] Several streets were renamed in honor of semi-legendary or mythical characters such as Karasaj batyr and Korkyt Ata or commemorated places which were symbolically important for the pre-Soviet Kazakhstan. These were Bayanauyl, Otrar, Taraz, Sary-Arka, Syrdarya and so on.

The appropriation of Lev Gumiljov's name may help to understand Kazakhstan's contemporary foreign policy. The Eurasian National University in Astana was established on the site of the former Akmola Pedagogic Institute. Previously named in honor of playwright Saken Seifullin, in 2001 it was renamed in honor of historian Lev Gumiljov, known for his insightful research on the ancient Turks. The initiative to perpetuate Gumiljov, associated with the doctrine of "Eurasian" economic and political integration, came directly from president Nazarbayev. Since the

---

253 The Second World War is called the Great Patriotic War in Kazakhstan, according to the Soviet tradition. This situation is not the same in other post-Soviet countries. Uzbekistan, for instance, claims that it participated in The Second World War on the side of the Soviet Union.
254 In fact, both mean "peace," but the second one is spelled in Kazakh.

Figure 5.4 A list with selected former and current street names in Astana. (Created by Nari Shelekpayev).

Current name	Former name
Bukeihan	Sacco i Vanzetti
Zhubanov	Lihachev
Akžaiyk	Monin
Bejbitshilik	Mir
Birzhan Sal	Vokzalnij
Dulati	Socialisticheskij
Kenesary	Karl Marx
Gumiljov	Kravcov
Mahtumkuly	Stroitelnyj
Otrar	Ordzhonikidze
Tlendiev	Astrahanskij
Syrdarja	Mikoyan
Taraz	Grekov
Tattimbet	Valihanov
Ualihanov	Avdeed
Baisekova	Rabochij

1990s, Nazarbayev has been a fervent supporter of Eurasian integration, which meant, in political terms, close economic and political cooperation with Russia. Since the late 1990s, he constantly evoked Lev Gumiljov in his writings.[255] Thus, one may observe how Kazakhstan's street-naming witnessed a turn-about from a close cooperation with Turkey, which shared no common borders and few common geopolitical interests with Kazakhstan, to Eurasianism and political rapprochement with Russia, with which the country shared a *lingua franca*, borders, and common economic and political interests. Interestingly, another national university opened in Astana ten years later, created from scratch, it was named in honor of Nazarbayev himself.

If common features in the street-naming of the two cities are useful for understanding the process of nation-building in general, differences say a lot about the level of resistance of local identities and the impor-

255 See Nursultan Nazarbayev, *Evraziiskii sojuz: idei, praktika, perspektivi, 1994–1997*, Moskva: Fond Sodeistviu Politicheskikh i Socialnikh Nauk 1997; Nursultan Nazarbayev, *Epicenter of Peace*, Hollis, NH: Puritan Press 2001.

tance of local memories. When one compares Astana and Almaty, more streets dedicated to local citizens can be found in the latter. At the same time, it is not a rare thing both in Astana and Almaty that local citizens do not know whom their streets commemorate. People frequently acknowledge that they are far from being familiar with all street names in their home city. One should also bear in mind the "structural" differences between two cities. Almaty has an important number of long-term residents who love their city and are willing to participate in its political, social, and cultural life. Astana has recently become home for many people (who may still keep strong ties with their native cities) whose feeling of belonging and appropriation of space have not yet crystallized. Does the name of a street really matter if one only crosses it going home from the office during weekdays and leaves the city for the week-end? Whether the weak ties between Astana and its inhabitants would eventually evolve into a different relationship is an open question.

Conclusion

Naming is a complex process and identifiable modifications in its evolution can reveal information not only about the past of a place but also about its present. If the purpose of place-naming is to "naturalize a certain ideology," as theorized by Rose-Redwood, in Astana and Almaty this process sought to do this through the elaboration of certain historical continuities. These continuities highlighted some "dark places" and characters from a pre-Soviet past, and, at the same time, introduced a new hierarchy in the system of urban coordinates. However, in some cases the introduction of the new signs caused discontinuities depending on perception and challenged the collective memory of those people who felt a nostalgia for the Soviet Union. "The less memory is experienced from the inside the more it exists only through its exterior scaffolding and outward signs," wrote Pierre Nora.[256] The renaming of streets became what Bourdieu called a "magical act" through which new signs or places of memory were established. However, the "magic" of these newly established lieux lasted only until the moment when routine destroyed a cognitive dissonance resulting from the interaction of human beings and the unknown signs to which they were exposed and which intruded on the previous system of coordinates. For it is the routine, and not the

---

256 Nora 1989, p. 13.

state ideology, that wipes down the active and fresh perception of the sign's novelty, making the perception of it into something passive and mechanical.

Place-naming is subject to change, and any substantial change of ideology or political transformation may hypothetically inspire a wish to reshape or reconsider the existing names, simply because it is easier to rename than to rebuild. At present, the street-renaming in Astana and Almaty is mainly characterized by a "primordial" rediscovery of the seventeenth, eighteenth and nineteenth centuries and a certain evisceration of the Soviet collective memory from the urban text of Kazakhstan's two main cities. It may also be concluded that the desire to promote a certain vision of the past and render this vision self-evident is attained through a process, which despite its apparent spontaneity and inconsistencies, had a number of identifiable features.

Skopje 2014: The Role of Government in the Spatial Politics of Collective Memory

Ivana Nikolovska

Introduction

In February 2010, the project *Skopje 2014* was finally unveiled to the Macedonian public. A flagship project of the national government, the scheme envisaged a grandiose (re)construction of the Skopje city centre. The government declared a new, distinctively "European", image of the city as the main aim of the project. Within four years, the capital city witnessed the appearance of dozens of new representative buildings and a number of monuments, as well as the reconstruction of several older urban structures. The materialization of the plan was accompanied by an outburst of public controversies and critical reactions to the project in Macedonian public discourse. It is the political meanings inscribed in the urban public space – or read into it – that is the main focus of this chapter. *Skopje 2014* serves as a case study that epitomizes the conditions of post-socialist Skopje and Macedonia (or FYROM) at large. After briefly discussing the theoretical background, the chapter will proceed with a short account of the historical context. The main part will focus on the conflicting views, looking at the position of the authors of the project as well as the opinions of those who accepted the project and those who opposed it. The study thus examines texts that appeared in public discourse and makes use of interviews conducted by the author on the spot with users of the city.[257]

---

257 My engagement with this project started with ethnographical observations on the statue of the Warrior on a Horse, unofficially known as Alexander the Great. At first, I concentrated on the political dispute between the Republics of Macedonia and Greece on the use of the name Macedonia and of the symbols relating to Alexander the Great and the Ancient Macedonian Kingdom, which, according to Greek interpretation, only the Greeks have the exclusive right to use. Further, my interest shifted to the matter of the fabrication of a nation by interpreting

Theoretical Background

The theme is rather complex: it touches on the past, both previous urban development and the reinvented history of the nation, as conveyed by the new architecture; it relates to space and its meaning, as the project *Skopje 2014* is basically a spatial undertaking; and it is crucially linked to the perceptions, attitudes and values of a people. For those reasons, a multi-dimensional approach is needed, which combines a historic method with an analysis of space and public debates. In terms of theory, *Skopje 2014* can be approached through various concepts, such as the social space and urban semiotics, nation branding, the invention of tradition, and collective memory.

The political dimension of (urban) space became a commonplace among critical urban scholars. As Henri Lefebvre famously argued, every space is socially produced and thus subject to a critical analysis that can reveal power relations behind the space formation.[258] Scholars in urban semiotics too have claimed that urban space – as well as its elements – can be decoded as a system of signs that is fundamentally formed by social struggles.[259] While most spaces bear traits of a plenitude of acts, interests, and signifying processes, and are thus literally "overwritten" with different meanings, some spaces have been designed as monumental spaces with a clear political message.[260] *Skopje 2014* is just one in many cases, where politicians tend to use public space as a tool for promoting specific visions and influencing public opinion, and, from the perspective of urban semiotics, for creating an overarching, hegemonic image of the city.[261] As the case of *Skopje 2014* makes clear, the political use of public spaces often manipulates collective narratives. Those are however usually particular, as they represent the memory of specific groups of people, or the elites, rather than an all-embracing memory of the whole society. Besides, the meanings of the particular monuments may be ambiguous. These perspectives open many questions. After the project *Skopje 2014* is completed, what can a researcher or a traveller understand

symbols, to arrive finally at the point of research into all the symbols and historical figures that are represented in the project *Skopje 2014*.

258 Henri Lefebvre, *The Production of Space*, Cambridge (Mass.): Basic Blackwell 1991.
259 Mark Gottdiener – Alexandros Lagopoulos (eds.), *The City and the Sign: An Introduction to Urban Semiotics*, New York: Columbia University Press 1986.
260 Lefebvre 1991, p. 143.
261 Mark Gottdiener, "Culture, Ideology, and the Sign of the City," in: Gottdiener – Lagopoulos 1986, p. 207.

from the city as a historical source when decoding it? How may one interpret the statues with hidden names and gigantic shapes in project *Skopje 2014*? For instance, the statue "Warrior on a Horse" unofficially represents Alexander the Great, whom myths represent as bisexual. As one commentator pointed out, his statue was erected in a very conservative and homophobic society.[262]

Tradition and memory are two other concepts that help us in understanding the sources of controversy over *Skopje 2014*. Several dissonances arise, such as the incongruence between the existing architectural heritage, conceived of as a source of distinct urban identity and a genuine tradition, and the new, "invented tradition" of neobaroque and neoclassical architecture that can hardly find any meaningful placement in the past and that overshadows important layers of urban heritage (especially Ottoman and socialist). Eric Hobsbawm defined the invention of tradition as a set of practices that are symbolic in nature and that aim at inculcating certain values and norms, which would imply continuity with the past.[263] The aim of the Macedonian government is precisely to create a long and continuous history of the Macedonian nation. Yet while this is not unique in European nation building, the question is how far the process of invention can go in the selection and the re-appropriation of the old materials, so that the fabricated tradition becomes popularly accepted rather than contested – or even resented – as too artificial a construction. What comes prominently to the fore in the critiques of *Skopje 2014* is precisely the perceived tension between the existing architectural heritage of the city and the newly constructed architectural styles and monuments, promoted by the government as the new heritage. The effort to erase a part of history or revise it and change the material evidence that belonged to a previous regime is a typical reaction of post-socialist countries. In this particular case, a need for a new identity goes along with a highlighted tendency to historicism. All countries striving for such a change tend to apply new sets of aesthetic principles by erasing what can be erased from the previous system.

Besides dislike of the new tradition, a more fundamental problem of memory dissonance or even clashes is at stake. This can be conceptualized as the tension between the officially endorsed collective memory

262 Jasna Koteska, "Troubles with History: Skopje 2014," *ARTmargins Online*, 29 December 2011. Accessible at: http://www.artmargins.com/index.php/2-articles/655-troubles-with-history--skopje-2014. Last retrieved 5 December 2015.
263 Eric Hobsbawm – Terence Ranger (eds.), *The Invention of Tradition*, Cambridge: Cambridge University Press 1983.

Figure 6.1 Skopje, Macedonia – Art Bridge, Financial Police Office and Ministry of Foreign Affairs buildings, 2014.
Source: Pudelek, Wikimedia Commons.

that, ultimately, tends to represent a particular ethno-history, and the particular group memories (e.g., of the ethnicities living in Macedonia), or even individual ones, which find themselves obscured or removed from the urban space. The public space of the capital cities is a powerful means through which the symbolic representation of the political order is expressed; yet this representation has to compete with layers of alternative memories – and identities – that are inscribed in the urban space.[264] Alternatively, we can apply the well-known conceptual distinction, coined by Jan Assmann, between the "cultural" memory and the "communicative" (or everyday) memory.[265] The communicative memory – which is transferred informally and limited temporally to a horizon of three generations – includes a variety of collective memories that are based on everyday communications. Via these reciprocal interactions, the

264 Moritz Csáky, "Introduction," *Collective Identities in Central Europe in Modern Times*, Moritz Csáky – Elena Mannová (eds.), Bratislava: Institute of History of the Slovak Academy of Sciences 1999, pp. 7–22.

265 Jan Assmann, "Collective Memory and Cultural Identity," *New German Critique* 65 (Spring – Summer 1995), pp. 125–133; Jan Assmann, Communicative and Cultural Memory, in: *Cultural Memory Studies. An International and Interdisciplinary Handbook*, Astrid Erll – Ansgar Nünning (eds.), Berlin – New York: de Gryuter 2008, pp. 109–118.

individuals compose a memory, which is always socially mediated and which relates to a social group. Since every individual belongs to numerous groups (such as family, neighborhood, profession, and nation), he or she may embrace various collective memories. The cultural memory, to the contrary, transcends the horizon of lived memory and it becomes objectivised in cultural items such as text, images, rites, buildings, monuments, cities, and even landscapes. The preservation and transmission of cultural memory is secured by professionals and by specialized institutions. Though disconnected from the sphere of everyday communication, the cultural memory is no less relevant for the identity of the collective. Quite to the contrary, "the group bases its consciousness of unity and specificity upon this knowledge and derives formative and normative impulses from it, which allows the group to reproduce its identity."[266] Seen in this perspective, *Skopje 2014* is a perfect example of the effort to objectivize in stone a cultural memory, which is supposed to preserve or reproduce the particular identity of the new nation state and to give formative and normative impulses to the residents of Skopje. Yet their communicative memory seems to be at odds with this version of cultural memory and it can be different from resident to resident as well, as it is conditioned by belonging to various social groups and identities that are formed in interactions and transferred from generation to generation.

Finally, we can use the concept of "nation branding" for the interpretation of *Skopje 2014*. According to the anthropologist Andrew Graan, the project has served as a strategic tool for the Macedonian government to fabricate a new image of the state. One of the major objectives was to attract investors and tourists on the global market via the new image, and thus encourage the economic development of the country, although there were other rationales at stake, too, such as increasing legitimacy vis-à-vis neighboring Greece and Albanian secessionist challenges.[267] Akin to Graan, I adopt the hypothesis that the Macedonian Government is branding the city and promoting the nation in order to further economic development and also to fabricate the image of the city for promoting Macedonians as a nation with a long established tradition. The government fosters, as it claims, the European identity of Skopje. Yet the

266 Assmann 1995, p. 128.
267 Andrew Graan, "Counterfeiting the Nation? Skopje 2014 and the Politics of Nation Branding in Macedonia," *Cultural Anthropology* 28, no. 1 (2013), pp. 161–179. For a similar perspective, see also Sabina Cvitković – Mihael Kline: "Skopje: Rebranding the Capital City through Architecture and Monuments to Remake the Nation Brand," *Sociologija i prostor* 55, no. 1 (2017), pp. 33–53.

branding of the city into one more Europeanized opens many questions: What is the content of European identity? What is the meaning of Europeanization and how does it correlate with the national content of the project *Skopje 2014*? Are the two identities presented as contradictory or complementary? How does the public perceive these identities?

The Macedonian architect Boris Chipan pointed out that the construction of a city can be influenced by emotional and social relationships, which may later become a narrative of tangible and intangible traditions. He claimed that architecture testifies to problems in the urban solution of creating a unique city. Cities are becoming more and more similar to one another and they lose their authenticity in the form of a tangible link with the past.[268] This argument supports my thesis that by making the image of the city a more Europeanized one through a re-interpretation of urban space, *Skopje 2014* negatively affects the tangible and intangible local traditions of the city. The Europeanization of the image of Skopje overshadows the Ottoman oriental look of the city and the layer of architecture from the twentieth century, including the much-valued brutalism, by adding objects that merely simulate the typical objects to be found in cities such as Paris, Rome, or Venice.

Urban Development of Skopje

In order to understand the critical comments that have surrounded the project *Skopje 2014*, a brief overview of the history of Skopje is instructive. The focus will be on architectural and urban development, which will be traced through the various periods in history, defined by the rule of different empires. This will also help us to see how the distinct architectural identity of the city evolved, which may be characterized as a cluster of multiple layers of history.[269]

Skopje is located in northern Macedonia below Mount Vodno. The city is divided by the upper reaches of the River Vardar. Skopje covers a territory of 571.46 km^2 and it has got 506,926 inhabitants according to the last census held in 2002. But it is believed that the population of the city population has actually grown to around one million. The exact number is unknown since the last census planned for 2012 was cancelled. The majority of the inhabitants are Macedonians (65%), followed

268 Boris Chipan, *Makedonskite gradovi vo XIX vek i nivnata urbana perspektiva*, Skopje: Makedonska Akademija na Naukite i Umetnostite 1987.
269 For a concise profile of the city, see Stefan Bouzarovski, "Skopje," *Cities* 28 (2011), pp. 265–277.

by Albanians (25%), Turks, Bosnians, Roma people and other minorities. The central position of Macedonia in the Balkan Peninsula gave the city a considerable regional importance, both nowadays and in the past. The city lies in the historically dynamic region between Central Europe and the Aegean Sea. Therefore, the fabric of the city was always reorganized to represent the rule of those who had conquered it.

As regards the etymology, the name Skopje is derived from the name Scupi, which dates back to the period of the Roman Empire. The first urban structure of Scupi consisted of buildings with paved streets and squares, thermal baths with a first-rate water management system. Scupi was a Latinized administrative unit of the Eastern Roman Empire. During the Middle Ages, the city successively belonged to Bulgarian and Serbian realms. The name was changed to Üsküp when the Ottomans captured the city and transformed it into a military base and a market venue where they traded slaves. In 1555 a devastating earthquake destroyed the eminent Christian architecture of the city. The Ottomans continued to build in their own Ottoman style; first they built a new working zone called *Čaršija*, a street with a market place and with trading shops.

Figure 6.2 Old Town (Carsija) Scene – Skopje – Macedonia, 2013.
Source: Adam Jones, Wikimedia Commons.

The importance of this zone brought it to the attention of merchants and travellers, such as Arabs, Jews, Greeks and Venetians. As a consequence of the establishment of the railway track, the urban development of Üsküp grew and residents settled on the southern riverbank. In 1888 the railway tracks were extended to Kumanovo and Niš, which spread the urban development even more in the southern part below the River Vardar. The architecture of Uskup gained an Ottoman look due to the construction of mosques. The buildings that have remained from that period are, among others, the Sultan Murat Mosque, the Clock Tower, the Fortress Kale, the Stone Bridge, the work zone called *Čaršija* (Old Town), the Turkish baths – the Daut Pasha Hammam – and the Burmali Mosque.[270] The symbolic image of the *hammam*, mosques and the working zone *Čaršija* gave the city the specific character of a religious, clean, and industrious place. The churches that remained during the Ottoman period had an important meaning for Christians – for them they maintained their identity thanks to which they started nation-building activities against the Ottomans. One of the urban values that have remained from this period is the residential zone and the structure of the municipalities, called *Maalo*. Among the ones that are still preserved to this day are *Madzir Maalo, Chair, Pajko Maalo*, and the *Evrejsko Maalo*. The streets have an irregular flow that resulted from the spontaneous development of the urban network, which referred to the natural development of the areas inspired by the Ottoman organization of cities. The municipalities were inhabited by a mixed population of Muslims, Christians, and Jews, who were organized in communities administered by their religious representatives. Each community had a central tap, a bakery, and a massive tree that would provide shade and would also function as a central meeting place for the residents. Apart from religious activities, residents did not have any other cultural activities.[271]

At the end of the nineteenth- and the beginning of the twentieth-century, the Ottoman Empire had to face serious economic and political problems. The politically autonomous units were undermined by the Christians who were strengthened and emancipated as a result of the uprisings. Furthermore, the church played an important role as a core base for the revival of educational activities and the stimulation of nation building movements against the Ottomans.[272]

---

270 Milan Mijalkovic – Katharina Urbanek, *Skopje, the World Bastard: Architecture of the Divided City*, Klagenfurt: Wieser Verlag 2011.

271 Chipan, 1987.

272 Mijalkovic – Urbanek 2011.

The medieval city of Skopje was characterized by architectural features such as churches, *hammams*, mosques, and a fortress. These elements remained a monumental reality until the nineteenth century. When Western influence arrived in the region, it affected the architecture and was signified by the construction of post-offices, schools and city-halls. This also reflected the social and political changes taking place in the Ottoman Empire.[273]

In 1912, Albanian rebels took over Uskup from the Ottoman Empire and made the city a part of Great Albania. In the same year, the Balkan War broke out and ended a year later with the signing of the Bucharest Treaty. The Ottomans were ousted from the Balkans and the territory of modern Macedonia was divided among Serbians, Bulgarians and Greeks. The city of Üsküp belonged to Serbia but desire for the territory by its covetous neighbours resulted in several clashes at battlefronts during World War I. The territory of contemporary Macedonia was included in the Yugoslav state in 1918 as part of the Kingdom of Serbia. In 1929, Yugoslavia was subdivided into administrative units called "banovinas." Skopje became the capital of the Vardar Banovina, which covered Macedonia, but also parts of southern Serbia and present-day Kosovo. The name Üsküp was changed to Skoplje and in the following years, the territory of the city did not increase. In 1931, about 68,000 inhabitants were registered in the city. The city acquired a new architectural image in the neoclassical style as opposed to the archetypical Ottoman style. The Burmali Mosque was torn down and replaced by the Officer Club. Besides, the new National Bank and the National Theatre were also built in a neoclassical style and they formed the square devoted to King Petar the Great.[274]

During World War II Skoplje was conquered by the Bulgarians and the city witnessed another change of monuments when the symbols of previous rulers were replaced and the city was renamed from Skoplje to Skopie. The Bulgarians built new museums, libraries, schools, a theatre, and a university devoted to Tsar Boris. Furthermore, at the end of 1944 the *Partizans*, led by Josip Broz Tito, adopted the territory of present-day Macedonia and for the first time, the foundations for Macedonian statehood were established as the Macedonian Republic with its own Macedonian language was established as part of the federal system of Yugoslavia. The name of the city evolved into the current version Skopje. As

273 Chipan 1987.
274 Mijalkovic – Urbanek 2011.

the largest city, it naturally became the capital and acquired appropriate administrative, economic and cultural functions. The national square in Skopje was renamed and dedicated to Marshal Tito, while the monuments of the former regime were melted down and replaced with symbols of National Freedom. The city of Skopje grew in size, as did the number of residents, which rose from 82,000 in 1945.[275]

On 26 July 1963, a catastrophic earthquake completely destroyed around 70% of the city of Skopje. One of the architects who worked on the urban solution for the city centre of Skopje was the Japanese architect Kenzo Tange, well-known for the reconstruction of Hiroshima. Tange considered the city as a structure that should correspond to the functions of a society. In the case of Skopje, he suggested two main elements: the city wall and the city port. The first element consisted of a dense residential zone designed for around thirty thousand inhabitants. Regarding the second element, the city port, Tange planned features with public functions such as the railway station and the bus station. He called the riverbank the nucleus of the city and he planned the construction of a telecommunications building and the siting of the post office there. He also planned the construction of two central squares, one on either side of the river. The first would be called the Square of Freedom and the second the Square of Marshal Tito. One of the essential parts of his plan was the building of Market House Bridge, which was to connect the old and the new part of the city. Tange's plan changed several times but most of his suggestions were accepted. However, the so-called nucleus of his plan never became a connecting zone and has remained an empty urban zone to this day. Regarding the two proposed squares, only one of them was realized and that was the square devoted to Marshal Tito, which today is Macedonia Square. The other planned square remains an empty zone and is used as an unofficial Roma market.[276]

After the break-up of Yugoslavia in 1991, the city of Skopje remained the capital of the newly established independent Republic of Macedonia. The former centralized administrative governance of the city was reorganized. The experience of an independent state brought new issues, such as the promotion of Macedonian identity. For instance, the core symbols of the Republic of Macedonia were regarded with disapproval by neighboring states. The Macedonian language was considered by Bulgarians

275 Ibid.
276 Ibid.

to be a Bulgarian dialect. The new flag and the name Macedonia caused issues for the Greeks who claimed these symbols as part of their Hellenistic heritage.

The importance of these symbols became a significant part of the struggle of Macedonian politicians for promoting the new nation-state identity. Interrelations among ethnic groups became more and more tense, especially relations between ethnic Albanians and ethnic Macedonians. The actions that shaped those relations started in 1994 when the first private Albanian university was opened. At that time, the newly adopted laws on decentralization and the reorganization of local units and their delegacies irritated Albanians who criticized them as discriminatory and mono-ethnically oriented, and the dispute led to brief military interventions at three different places where radical ethnic Albanians confronted Macedonian state forces. In the same year, the Ohrid Frame Agreement was signed which meant that tensions ceased and better rights for ethnic minorities were secured in order to contribute to a more functional process of decentralization and autonomy on a local level. A similar labeling of public places occurred in Skopje in 2002 when situating a seventy-seven meter high millennium cross on top of the hill of Vodno. In consequence, the Albanian community erected a statue of the Albanian warrior Skenderbeg in the centre of Skopje in 2007.[277]

As the overview of the development of Skopje from the *longue durée* perspective makes clear, *Skopje 2014* is not the only attempt at modernization and Europeanization articulated for Skopje. Fabio Mattioli points out three main phases. The first wave came with the establishment of the Kingdom of Yugoslavia, which brought about de-Ottomanization and a modernization of the cities with the aim to make them look European and Occidental. The second wave arrived during reconstruction after WWII, and especially after the earthquake in 1963. The reconstruction proposed by Kenzo Tange can also be understood as a way to modernize and Occidentalize the city. The project *Skopje 2014* introduced by the Macedonian government highlighted the national interpretation and appropriation of the European tradition in architecture and the building of cities.[278]

---

277 Goran Janev, "Narrating the Nation, Narrating the City," *Cultural Analysis* 10 (2011), pp. 3–21.
278 Fabio Mattioli, "Unchanging boundaries: the reconstruction of Skopje and the politics of heritage," *International Journal of Heritage Studies* 20, no. 6 (2014), pp. 599–615.

Project *Skopje 2014*

The project *Skopje 2014* covered the construction and reconstruction of buildings and monuments in the capital city of Skopje and was planned to be accomplished by the year 2014.[279] Financial responsibility for the project was laid in the hands of the Macedonian government which represented the ideology of the ruling party *Vnatreshna Makedonska Revolucionerna Organizacija - Demokratska Partija za Makedonsko Nacionalno Edinstvo* (VMRO-DPMNE).

The scheme was unveiled in 2010, using a 3D visualization of the future look of the centre of the city and figured on state television, in the media, and on the internet. About twenty new buildings and around forty new monuments devoted to historical figures were announced. As regards the former, the project envisaged new buildings for cultural institutions such as a national theatre, a museum of archaeology, a museum featuring the Macedonian struggle for independence, and a Macedonian philharmonic orchestra hall. Furthermore, several new government buildings were planned, such as one for the Ministry of Finance, the Criminal Court, the Ministry of Foreign Affairs, and the Old and New City Halls. In addition, the project included the construction of bridges across the River Vardar, such as the Art Bridge, a pedestrian bridge with twenty-nine sculptures; and the Eye Bridge, another pedestrian bridge which would have twenty-eight sculptures. Part of the project covered existing bridges that were to be renovated, such as the Freedom Bridge; the Gotse Delchev Bridge, and the Revolution Bridge. Among the buildings to be renovated were the Houses of Parliament with new domes on the top. The Government building was to be renovated into baroque style with a new façade. Some residential buildings in the city centre are also under façade reconstruction. Other segments of the project included the construction of Skenderbeg Square, the creation of fountains in the River Vardar and the embedding of two boats anchored on the riverside – one of the boats already operates as a restaurant called Royal Boat Macedonia – and the construction of parking lots and hotels.

Regarding monuments, it was proposed to erect around forty new statues, such as Justinian I, Mother Teresa, a pavilion at Macedonia Square, an Arch Macedonia, Tsar Samuil, the statue of a warrior to rep-

---

279 In fact, many buildings were still under construction at the beginning of the year 2016 when this volume was being finalized. SkenderBeg Square was not finished and some residential buildings were under façade construction.

Figure 6.3 Samuil monument in Skopje, 2011.
Source: Dalco26, Wikimedia Commons.

resent Philip II, and a statue with the official name "Warrior on a Horse,"
though unofficially it represents Alexander the Great. Others were meant
to represent prominent figures in Macedonian history, such as the saints
Cyril and Methodius, and the statues of their students, Naum and Kli-
ment, as well as heroes from the time of the Ottoman Empire, both World
Wars, and important figures in the building of the nation and the state.

Individuals who strove for the independence of the Republic during the communist regime in Yugoslavia were also included on the list.

The 3D visualization resulted in a stunned reaction. The first presentation in February 2010 was perceived as the type of massive political campaign that usually occurs before elections. There was a conviction that project *Skopje 2014* had been received positively. Yet, after three years, when this study was written, the citizens of Skopje were puzzled by the definition and the goals of the project, and they remain puzzled even today, six years after the campaign. Instead of promoting interest in architecture and concentrating on urban development, the project has only provoked tensions and altercations among politicians and ethnicities.

Comments and Criticism Regarding Project *Skopje 2014*

The massive urban renovation plan for the city faced a polarized reception.[280] There were many supporters who admired the plan and praised it as a positive effort by the government to remake Skopje into a "Europeanized" capital which would attract more visitors and promote the development of the tourism industry. On the other hand, opponents of the project have offered numerous arguments against it. The project has been criticized for being too expensive, with an estimated cost of around eighty to five hundred million Euros. Moreover it has been claimed that the attempt at the so-called "antiquisation" of the city creates tensions among ethnic groups living in the Republic, such as Albanians, Turks, Serbs, and Roma. For example, the proportion of monuments is not balanced in such a way as to adequately narrate the presence of ethnic Albanians in the state, with the exception of the statues of Skenderbeg and Mother Teresa. Also, the project exacerbates bilateral relations with neighboring Greece, which has already disputed the name of the state, as demonstrated by Greek politicians declaring that Greece has the exclusive right to the use of symbols referring to the ancient Kingdom of Macedonia, especially Alexander the Great and the name Macedonia. The main objection by students, architects and intellectuals to the project was based on the argument that it will distort the image of the city and

---

280 The overview of the attitudes and arguments is based on my survey of several media and platforms that covered *Skopje 2014*, especially various internet portals, including some foreign ones, as well as of printed publications that focused on the project. For more details, see Ivana Nikolovska, *Skopje2014: Governmental Role in the Spatial Politics of Collective Memory*, unpublished master thesis, Prague: Charles University 2013.

the memories of its residents by overshadowing the Ottoman heritage that has survived from the period of Ottoman rule, and which is considered part of the typical architectural style of the city.

The project was launched by Prime Minister Nikola Gruevski. He used the occasion of the official opening of the Arch Macedonia (*Porta Makedonija*) on 6 January 2011 to address a larger audience in his first public speech on *Skopje 2014*. In his speech, he stated with confidence: "I have supported and continue to support the project, as I always do when believing in something: ideas, visions, for the welfare of the citizens. This gathering is a triumph for the nation, the state and independence."[281] After expressing thanks to all the project's supporters, and also making a gesture of appreciation to various opponents of the project, such as the political opposition, NGO's, and some of the critical intellectuals, the prime minister highlighted the social-economic aspect of the project as well as its prospectively unifying effect:

> "It is important to remember that this project has not only enabled the survival of a large number of construction companies, but also of over 10,000 workers in a period of the most serious global crisis. [...] After our departure, the works of art will remain to glow with all of their splendor, enabling future generations, unburdened by the manipulation of political parties, to present their opinion."[282]

Following the Prime Minister's speech, the Minister of Culture Elizabeta Kancheska-Milevska added that the Arch symbolizes the great victory of Macedonian civilization, by which she meant the establishment of the independent state: "Our motto [is] that we understand the world solely as a field for cultural competition among nations. [...] I wish for the Arch Macedonia to become a monumental book of Macedonia's accomplishments, the place where, as great Goethe said, art will be a mediator of everything that may not be expressed with words."[283]

We can interpret the Minister of Culture's speech as an attempt to articulate Macedonia's contribution to European civilization and to peaceful competition on the global stage. She also tried to build a bridge between national and European identity, while emphasizing the sense of

---

281 "PM Gruevski: Yes, Skopje 2014 Was My Idea," MINA: Macedonian International News Agency, 7 January 2012, Skopje. Accessible at: http://macedoniaonline.eu/content/view/20045/45/. Last retrieved 9 April 2013.

282 Ibid.

283 Ibid.

Figure 6.4 Triumphal arch "Porta Macedonia" in Skopje, Macedonia, 2012.
Source: Rašo, Wikimedia Commons.

prestige stemming from belonging to the Macedonian nation. Regarding the Arch, the minister underlined the universal meanings epitomized by the arts, thus making clear that the Arch contained nothing that could be argued about, although the Arch, twenty-one meters high and covered with reliefs carved in marble depicting scenes from Macedonian history, became one of the most controversial and criticized monuments of *Skopje 2014*. The architect Boris Chipan criticizes the symbolism of the arch because, in his opinion, the meaning of a triumphal arch is that it signifies the victory of glorious generals and military men who pass through the arch in a symbolic celebration of conquered territories. He states that in none of the historical scenes presented was victory for the Macedonian nation achieved, except for one, the victory against Nazism, and this refers to more recent history.[284]

The political background was evoked by the prime minister to oppose adversary political parties, whereas future generations were warned against being blinded by the conspiracies of opponents and to respect the significance of the arts. The ironic thanks addressed to opponents

284 Boris Chipan, "'Sk 2014' Ne e Del od Nasata Tradicija," *Nered i groteska*, (Edicija Gradot, Vol 1), Skopje: Templum – Plostad Sloboda 2010, pp. 18–24.

does not take from the criticism voiced against the project, apart from defending the fact that ten thousand workers were hired in *Skopje 2014* and that more and more new construction companies have come into being. This kind of speech can rather be seen as a judgment on those who think differently from the government. Moreover, such a speech can discourage present and future generations from being critical and make them more narrow-minded. This effect could actually be observed in Macedonia in the last decade. It was also symptomatic that those intellectuals and architects who did discuss *Skopje 2014* and its aesthetics in a critical manner could hardly do so without being marked as members of opposition political parties. It also seems that political parties in opposition have partly lost the ability to check and balance the ruling party.

Koce Trajanovski, the mayor of Skopje, defended the project arguing that Macedonia's capital needs an iconic hero who would brand the nation. He made a positive statement about the project in an interview for the Croatian National TV channel HRT. Drawing comparison between Croatian and Macedonian capital cities and the usable figures for symbolizing the nations, the mayor argued: "We have studied our history from the textbooks, but we never had anything to show or see. As the Croats placed a sculpture of Ban Jelacic on the central square in

Figure 6.5 Eye Bridge, 2013.
Source: Dennis Jarvis, Wikimedia Commons.

Zagreb, we also want to place on Skopje's main square something that is a symbol of our nation."[285] Alexander the Great, staged as the "Warrior on a Horse", was to play a role comparable to Josip Jelacic, the Croatian general and the military leader of the Croatian army during the revolution of 1848. Yet the statue "Warrior on a Horse" is one of the most controversial monuments erected in *Skopje 2014*. The adoption of Alexander the Great into the narrative of the Macedonian nation led many foreign media to criticize it as an attempt to provoke Greek politicians. Let us remember that the Republic of Greece has vetoed Macedonia's entry to NATO and prolonged negotiations for EU membership because it rejects the recognition of the name Macedonia. According to the Greeks it implies territorial intentions toward Greece; and, the use of symbols from the ancient Macedonian Empire is considered to be Greeks' exclusive right. Vasiliki Neofotistos, an anthropologist, made the point in connection with the statue "Warrior on a Horse:" "Macedonia wants to advance the thesis that it is a corner stone of Western Civilization."[286]

Besides the delicate Greek-Macedonian relations, critics also addressed the context of ethnic tension at home. Professor Miroslav Grchev put forward arguments that the project affects multi-ethnic relations and raises alarms on issues agreed to in the Ohrid Framework Agreement in 2001. For instance, the decision of the government to build a church on the square in Skopje is against Article 19 of the Constitution of the Republic of Macedonia and goes against the principles of the equal representation of religions by favoring the Macedonian Orthodox Church. Furthermore, he also pointed to a clash of competencies as regards the important figures. The so-called "Program for representing important historical figures and events", drawn up by the advisory body of the municipality, contradicts the Law of Memorial Statues. According to Article 4 of this law, historical figures of national significance fall within the jurisdiction of the National Assembly of the Republic of Macedonia. The monumental policy of the municipality, therefore, actually relegates the figures such as Gotse Delchev, a Macedonian ideologue from the period of the Ottoman Empire, to merely local significance.[287]

285 "FYROMian Skopje 2014, interview by Dragan Nikolic," 20 September 2011, Croatian National Television, accessible on Youtube: https://www.youtube.com/watch?v=ztL0uRmabhg. Last retrieved 10 December 2015.

286 Quoted in Matthew Brunwasser, "Macedonia Plays Up Past Glory," *The New York Times*, 23 June 2011. Accessible at: http://www.nytimes.com/2011/06/24/world/europe/24iht-macedonia24.html?pagewanted=all. Last retrieved 9 December 2015.

287 Miroslav Grchev, "Bezzakonie koe void do podelba na drzavata," *Gradat grad!*, (Edicija Gradot, Vol 2), Skopje: Templum – Plostad Svoboda 2010, pp. 87–95.

The relative weakness of civil society did not prevent concerted reactions. Among those who did not remain silent is the "First Archi Brigade" or *Prva Arhi Brigada* – PAB (*Protiv zidot na kichot*), a society of young architects from Skopje. They have put forward several arguments from an architectural, urban and infrastructural point of view. They think that several issues, totally ignored in the project, are the most important problems pertaining to *Skopje 2014*. The argument they offer refers to the "antiquisation" and use of the baroque style, which, when confronted with history and with the typical architectural styles used in Macedonia, has no relevance for Macedonian architecture and rather shows a frustration with and a lack of knowledge of indigenous and typical Macedonian architecture. They add that the proposed style of the parking lots is totally unacceptable in terms of engineering principles and also that the obelisk installed in the Women's Park does not respect the humanistic character of that park. Furthermore, they find the public competitions held by the Ministry of Culture faulty. The young architects claim the scheme the architect was supposed to follow had already been decided and that successful candidates simply accepted the template for the façades of buildings.[288]

Another professional platform of architects, The Association of Architects of the Republic of Macedonia (AAM) at its assembly devoted to *Skopje 2014* announced:

> "We, the architects, together with the citizens are positioned in a very inconvenient situation. The professional and the general public opinion are not integrated into the decision-making process for *Skopje 2014*. It is very important to express the opinion of those who critically comment on this project. Our thesis does not offer ready solutions but aims to open questioning and to develop a profound discussion in order to continue the procedure of negotiating and deciding. The AAM does not support the project *Skopje 2014* as it is because it lacks a temporal, geographic, political, economic, cultural and social context. It is professionally inconsistent. It does not indicate the future."[289]

The artists associated with the project, most of whom were previously unknown to the public and without any very striking portfolios, were crit-

---

288 PRVA ARHI-BRIGADA: "Protiv zidot na kichot," *Gradat grad!*, (Edicija Gradot, Vol 2), Skopje: Templum – Plostad Svoboda 2010, pp. 49–54.

289 Quoted in: "Predgovor," *Gradat grad!*, (Edicija Gradot, Vol 2), Skopje: Templum – Plostad Svoboda 2010, p. 7.

icized for their work on the monuments, and denounced for not having been chosen through fair and public competition. No wonder then that the accused artists, creators, and sculptors gathered in order to defend their work. The artist Aleksandar Stankovski, for instance, justified *Skopje 2014* with the argument that "the government represents the taste of the citizens who vote and thus made an aesthetic choice."[290] The sculptor Dimitar Filipovski, the creator of the statue of Metodija Andonov-Chento (the first Macedonian President) defended his work by saying that he supports humanistic and realistic art rather than modern art, which in his opinion is rather a quasi-art.[291] It can be assumed, however, that when architects are hired by the government, they may not feel free to express tastes and visions that would differ from what has been commissioned by the government.

Some of the critiques addressed the question of what message about the society and the government the monumental rebuilding actually conveys. Architect Miroslav Grchev, an ardent critic of *Skopje 2014*, claims that architecture in a way mirrors the development of a society and the type of regime which was in power during the respective period and points out this is particularly manifested in state buildings and monuments. He gives the example of autocratic societies where architecture is tangible material evidence of the spirit of the rulers. Architecture and monumental statues can be seen as gauges monitoring the level of despotic rule; they are witnesses that show how critical or narrow-minded a society is. In this line of reasoning, he finds many common traits between the Macedonian prime minister, the so-called Great Leader, and the reign of Adolf Hitler, and their power over architecture. Both of them incorporated patterns of monumental styles from the architecture of other epochs and had them expressed in gigantic structures and sculptures, the aim being to erase the immediate past and to create identification with a new super-state.[292] Freud's theory also contributes to the interpretation of megalomaniac architecture where it is seen as resulting from the inferiority of leaders and as typical of nations that were oppressed in the past. This helps to explain the sudden search for identity and the equally sudden love for classical antiquity. It should be noted, however,

---

290 Quoted in: Biljana Nestoroska, "'Skopje 2014' Artists Defend Their Projects," portal BalkanInsight, 6 May 2010. Accessible at: http://www.balkaninsight.com/en/article/skopje-2014-artists-defend-their-projects. Last retrieved 9 January 2016.

291 Ibid.

292 Miroslav Grchev, "Arhitektonska psihopatologija," *Gradat grad!*, (Edicija Gradot, Vol 2), Skopje: Templum – Plostad Svoboda 2010, pp. 9–14.

that the term "antiquisation" does not describe a project in its entirety since there are actually a wide range of historical times represented in the project, such as the Medieval and the Renaissance period, and also the monuments and architecture of the twentieth century. Zarko Trajanoski, an expert on human rights, added some irony to the debate, when making a comparison with the famous Hero square in Budapest. After the fall of the socialist regime in Hungary in 1989 all of the socialist-realist statues were located in the Park of Statues or Hero Square. Asking about where the monuments of *Skopje 2014* will be moved in the future, Trajanoski proposed an ironic solution: to create a Museum of Macedonian illusion.[293]

Irony is also implied in the nicknames used for Skopje. Antagonists of the project label the transformed capital as "a city of joke" or they use terms, such as: Legoland, Las Vegas or Disneyland to describe *Skopje 2014*. Jasna Koteska, a Macedonian philosopher, points out the Disneyland metaphor is frequently used in today's architecture dictionary as an insult or offense to architecture. In her article "Troubles with history", she nevertheless shows the project needs a more complex interpretation. In fact, the project oscillates between two poles: modernism and postmodernism, i.e., a nineteenth-century historical eclecticism that reflected the seriousness of the state and the late twentieth-century playful architecture that reflects a certain distance from self-centered history. Koteska builds her argument on the distinction developed by Italian philosopher Giorgio Agamben who elaborated the concepts of "diachrony" and "synchrony" as two opposing modes of relating to history. It is the former mode, one that privileges the past at the expense of the present, that describes the Macedonian Government's attitude. There is nothing ironic or self-distancing about the intentional meanings of *Skopje2014*, quite the contrary. Historical figures and monumental styles are employed to convey unequivocally serious message about Macedonia being a great and historical nation. The Disney metaphor is therefore used somewhat incorrectly, although, as Koteska makes clear, the irony comes up incidentally via a highly decorative style for quite utilitarian institutions. The dichotomy of diachrony and synchrony, or the feelings of national seriousness and a certain distance from ethnocentrism, is linked with an identity split among the Macedonian population that goes along generational lines. The project, according to Koteska, actually forces people

293 Zarko Trajanoski, "Antikomanija na palankata," *Gradat grad!*, (Edicija Gradot, Vol 2), Skopje: Templum – Plostad Svoboda 2010, pp. 45–48.

to make a decision about their relationship to the past, and about their being either Slavs or descendants of the ancient Macedonians, a thesis, which she supports with the polarized results of an opinion poll conducted in March 2010, which showed that 54% of citizens did not support *Skopje 2014* and 46% did.[294]

Many of the critical comments by architects were related to the local tradition of urbanism and issues of urban identity. The architect Sanja Jovanovik, for instance, argued that longevity of the existing architectural heritage is proof of its authenticity and of a durable urban identity, and warned against "applying personal interests in the fabrication of a new identity [as this] can create chaos that will lead to the loss of the image of the city while producing problems for future generations."[295] The re-labeled image of Skopje can play a problematic role for future generations since modifying history will make theirs different from the memories and narratives of their parents and grandparents. By such modification, the government, instead of filling a gap in history, will create a "buffer zone" between the collective memories of younger generations and those of their ancestors. Ivan Jovanovski hinted at the artificialness of the project, when stating that "*Skopje 2014* is a project that won't only undermine the local urban identity, but it is also an anti-product in relation to global attempts to promote ourselves as a country that is an eternal cradle for authentic city life, priceless art, unique aromas, and irreplaceable sights."[296] In a similar vein, the urban expert Jasmina Siljanovska claimed that *Skopje 2014* lowers the image of the city and its values by twisting its cultural identity and that this is characteristic of a newly-composed nation state which does not have continuity. She called *Skopje 2014* an eclectic project that assembles and interprets classical architectural elements in a strange way. It all looks like a collection of souvenirs from different spaces and times. She pointed out several problems in *Skopje 2014*, such as the location of monuments, their problematic artistic value and the selection of project features in public competitions, which, in her opinion, do not uphold the civil character of a square and do not respect the freedom of the citizens.[297] Last but not least, Boris Chipan argued for

294 Koteska 2011.

295 Sanja Ragenovik-Jovanovik, "Da go Skrshime Sopstvenoto Ogledalo," *Gradat grad*!, (Edicija Gradot, Vol 2), Skopje: Templum – Plostad Svoboda 2010, pp. 36–39.

296 Ivan Jovanovski, "Razubavizator, verzija 2014," *Nered i groteska*, (Edicija Gradot, Vol 1), Skopje: Templum – Plostad Sloboda, 2010, pp. 25–28.

297 Jasmina Siljanovska, "Duhovna Impotencija," *Nered i groteska*, (Edicija Gradot, Vol 1), Skopje: Templum – Plostad Sloboda 2010, pp. 29–34.

respecting the local urban tradition. From that perspective, he claimed that the Officers Hall, the building that disappeared after the 1963 earthquake, is something that should not be rebuilt within the framework of Skopje's makeover, since the building was built during the period of the Kingdom of Serbs, Croats and Slovenes (later the Kingdom of Yugoslavia), and as such cannot be considered part of Macedonian architecture. When searching for an example of the genuinely Macedonian architecture, one should better take the Government building from the 1970 or a typical house in the city of Ohrid which display modern features of architecture.[298]

Ethnographical Observation on Macedonia Square

As we can see from the previous debate, the professional audience came with a range of critical arguments. Yet, what does the project look like when seen from the perspective of the ordinary users of the city? In fact, the observation and interviews with fourteen people revealed a variety of attitudes toward the project. The interviews were conducted close to the "Warrior on a Horse" statue in Skopje, on 28 April 2012, at 3 o'clock p.m. Let us shortly summarize them.

The first two people interviewed were a 24-year-old man and a 23-year-old woman, both of Macedonian ethnicity and students at the Faculty of Economics. Even though I introduced myself and my motivation, I could see their hesitation in answering my question. Regarding my question on what they thought about *Skopje 2014*, they both looked at the statue, "Warrior on a Horse," and the man decided to speak in the name of both, describing the project as expressing the pride of the nation in being descendants of Alexander the Great.

The second person I talked to was a 23-year-old man, a student of Macedonian ethnicity. When asked how he felt about *Skopje 2014* he only stated that the project should have been undertaken a long time ago.

The third interviewed person was a retired man of Macedonian ethnicity. He refused to give his age, but presumably he was in his sixties or seventies. When I started asking him questions, he made sure I was not an agent of the government. After I gave information about myself and my motivations, he shared his point of view, seeing the project as a disaster. He also thought that "the government has many other import-

---

298 Chipan 2010.

ant activities to work on instead of spending money on useless statues." He concluded by claiming that he felt Macedonian rather than Slav or ancient Macedonian.

Another respondent was a man of Macedonian ethnicity, 50 years old and employed. He was talkative and felt very comfortable with my questions relating to the project. He stated that the project affirmed his feeling of belonging to the nation. He specified that we could not separate Slavs from ancient Macedonians because, according to his belief, the ethnicities were mixed. He expressed a feeling of pride when looking at the fountain of the "Warrior on a Horse," which un-officially represents Alexander the Great. When I asked about his opinion, regarding the use the symbols at the fountain that, despite having fewer than sixteen rays, apparently referring to the Vergina symbol – the subject of controversy between Macedonia and Greece – he answered: "It is a good political trick that protects us from negative critics."

Then I interviewed two women, both Macedonian and employed. They refused to tell their age but I assume they were in their fifties or sixties. Their feedback referred to their pride in belonging to such a "great nation of descendants of the ancient Macedonians."

A couple in their sixties, a husband and wife, both Macedonian and retired, were other respondents. They both agreed that *Skopje 2014* should have occurred earlier. They believed that the Macedonian nation should not renounce its history and that the project provided a visible connection with the past.

Another respondent was a 40-year-old employed man of Macedonian ethnicity. He freely shared his opinion that due to the geographical position of the Republic of Macedonia, Macedonians should surely consider the project as being part of the national biography. He noted he felt more like a Slav rather than a descendant of the ancient Macedonians. He remarked that nations are mixed and that Macedonians have a more exclusive right to identify with the ancient Macedonians than the Greeks.

A man, who was 28 years old, unemployed and belonging to Albanian ethnicity, stated that *Skopje 2014* was a nationalistic move by the Government of Macedonia. He also added that he admired the image of Alexander the Great and he understood it as normal that people would like to assimilate him into the biography of their nation.

Another person was a 30-year-old man, employed and belonging to Macedonian ethnicity. Upon my question, he claimed that there was a lack of academic support in statements, books, interviews, etc., in which opinions on the project could be expressed

Figure 6.6 Skopje_Warrior on a Horse, 2013.
Source: Andrzej Wójtowicz, Wikimedia Commons.

Then I interviewed a 23-year-old girl who studied architecture and belonged to Macedonian ethnicity. She said she felt ashamed of her colleagues who, in her opinion, obviously destroyed the image of what was typical Macedonian architecture when reflecting upon the history of the nation.

The last respondent was a 24-year-old man, a student of economics, who belonged to Macedonian ethnicity. He referred to *Skopje 2014* as a waste of money that should have been spent instead on investing in underdeveloped areas, especially in those with a high percentage of unemployment. He believed that the history of the Macedonian nation began in the eighteenth and nineteenth centuries and added that some statues were useless for the identity of the nation.

A very helpful source for my research on the project, and a very up-to-date source for my ethnographic observation, was my Facebook network. As regards the project *Skopje 2014,* and the sudden and numerous erections of monuments, a joke circulated on the Facebook network referring to the fact that monuments are being erected everywhere, and so they might even appear in your coffee at some central cafeteria. The literal meaning of the joke was like this: "Don't go to the city centre for a coffee because they might put a statue in your coffee."[299]

The fieldwork did not aspire to creating a strictly representative sample of respondents that would represent all social groups. The interviews can therefore bring only a general insight into reactions towards *Skopje 2014.* Keeping this limitation in mind, we can nevertheless draw some conclusions regarding the opinions of ordinary citizens about the project. First, a sort of split in identification took place, as it seems that people easily appropriated identification with Alexander the Great without compromising identification with the Slavs. Such a phenomenon can be explained by the long negation of the Republic of Macedonia and the dispute with Greece. Also, the high rate of unemployment in the state made people sensitive and reactive to political issues. Although negatively criticized by intellectuals, the residents of Skopje evidently enjoyed the fountain when spending time in the area, taking pictures or pursuing other activities. The interviews also indicate that the younger generation – such as students, especially if they are not familiar with architecture – is not much concerned with what renovation of the façades means or with the significance of the newly applied architectural styles. They seemed much more concerned about the making of the new image

---

299 "Ne odi vo centar na kafe, stavaat statui vo kafeto."

of the city. Older generations seemed to be more concerned about the political and economic background to the project.

Conclusion

The new state elites can choose various strategies for branding the capital cities. While for Astana the Kazakh government decided on hypermodern architecture (see chapter four); in the case of Skopje, the ruling Macedonian party opted for (postmodern) baroque. This chapter wished to present a closer look at the project *Skopje 2014*. It pointed out the underlying aims of the project, its uneasy relation with the architectural tradition of Skopje, and the nodal points of controversies. The core of the chapter focused on the mapping of basic arguments pro and contra the project, as formulated in public discourse by both initiators and opponents from the professional public. On the side of the proponents, the need for rebranding the city and nation as up-to-date, open, and distinctively European was an important motive. So was the need to create – and to imprint in the public space – a new historical narrative of the Macedonian nation that would emphasize its glory and ancientness. An overview of the opponent voices identified a set of critical arguments. We may summarize them as an unbalanced representation of different ethnic groups; a disregard of the local and valuable layers of architecture; corruption of the city's particular character; the introduction of an artificial, mimicking and alien tradition; the low (kitsch-like) artistic value of the project; and, a break with the living traditions of the inhabitants. On a deeper level, a sensed arrogance of power and a ludicrous national pomposity frustrated some of the critics. In spite of this critique, however, many people showed a positive attitude toward and acceptance of *Skopje 2014*, as the results of the collected interviews revealed. How can we interpret this fact? Only a larger horizon of time will allow us to assess the effect of the project in a long run. For the time being, the academic and public debates will continue regarding the public use of history through new constructions in public places. I hope this case study will contribute to the discussion.

Searching for Identity: the Cities of Tiraspol and Chisinau

Olga Niutenko

Introduction

The collapse of the Soviet Union caused a significant number of intractable problems. In addition to the general political and economic difficulties of the transition period, the central questions for the former Soviet republics included redefining the status of the centre and the regions, undetermined borders, and on-going conflicts based on previous migration policies. The process of declaring sovereignty over the territory of the new republics and the integration of ethnic minorities in the new states, often densely populated, became one of the most significant disputes in the post-Soviet period.

The case of Transnistria in the Republic of Moldova is one of the consequences of the collapse of the Soviet Union. Transnistria, which literally means "beyond the Dniester River," is a narrow strip in Moldova, located between the Ukrainian border on the east and the Dniester River on the west that includes a number of settlements, and the city of Bender. The area is 4,016 sq. km.[300] It is defined as an autonomous territory within Moldova and is not internationally recognized as a nation.[301] The population of Transnistria is 509,439 (2012).[302] There are three major ethnic groups: Moldovans (31.9%), Russians (30.4%), and Ukrainians (28.8%).[303]

---

300 *Statisticheskiy Yezhegodnik 2012* [Annual Statistical Report], Tiraspol: Ministerstvo ekonomiki Pridnestrov'ya 2012, p. 17.

301 Transnitria Definitions. Accessible at: http://www.wordnik.com/words/Transnistria. Last retrieved 7 May 2013.

302 Press-vypusk *Demograficheskaya aituatsiya v PMR za 2012 god* [Press Release "The Demographic Situation in TMR in 2012"], Tiraspol 2013, p. 1.

303 Country overview. Accessible at: http://mfa-pmr.org/index.php?newsid=389/. Last retrieved 7 May 2013.

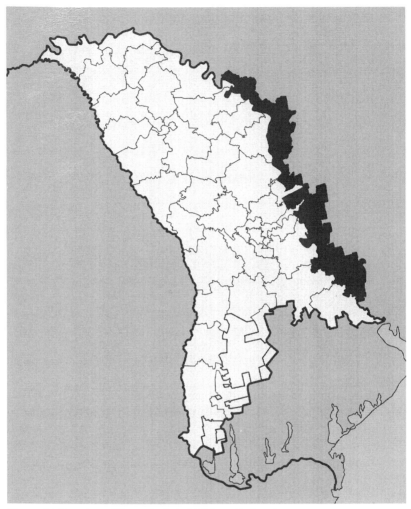

Figure 7.1 Location of Transnistria in Moldova (de facto).
Source: Wikimedia Commons.

Representing 75.8% of the population, the Moldovans are the most numerous nationality in the country as a whole. Ukrainians compose 8.4%,
Russians 5.9%, Gagauz 4.4%, Romanians 2.2%, Bulgarians 1.9%, and other nationalities 1.0% of the population, while 0.4% did not indicate their
nationality.[304]

---

304 *The Demographic Situation in TMR in 2012*, 2013, p. 19.

The "Law on the Functioning of Languages," which asserted the Romanian language as the state language of the Moldovan Soviet Socialist Republic (MSSR), was passed in 1989.[305] Subsequently, the law resulted in unrest among the Russian-speaking population of the MSSR. In 1990, the Transnistrian Moldovan Republic (TMR) proclaimed its independence, and since then it has sought international recognition. The situation that emerged influenced the rise of a nationalistic mood. Mass protest demonstrations in 1992 were suppressed by the Moldovan military resulting in thousands of deaths.[306]

The post-military period is characterized by the emergence of discussions on Transnistrian identity and statehood. This article examines the existence of Transnistrian identity through the lens of cities, using such markers of identity as language, education, and culture.[307]

Sovietness and Places of Memory

Was there a historic community called the "Soviet people" or is the phrase no more than an ideological slogan? Discussion of this question diminished sharply after the collapse of the Soviet Union. However, a new battle for "Soviet" identity began in the early 1990s, and one of the strongest proponents of Soviet identity was the unrecognized Transnistrian Moldovan Republic.

While some Soviet republics started separation on the basis of nationality, self-identity in Transnistria was more complicated. Ethnic aspects were too weak to be the reason for the secession of the TMR from the MSSR since the population of the region consisted of three approximately equal ethnic groups: Moldovans, Russians, and Ukrainians. Motives were more understandable in terms of culture – people protested against the new Moldovan law "On language" – and the economic and political program. Uniting against Romanianization, the Transnistrian authorities were not able to rely on an ethnic factor. Possibly the legacy of the

---

305 Zakon Nr. 3465 ot 01.09.1989, *O funktsionirovanii yazykov na territorii Mioldavskoy SSR* [The Law "On the Functioning of Languages in the MSSR"]. Accessible at: http://lex.justice.md/viewdoc .php?action=view&view=doc&id=312813&lang=2. Last retrieved 29 April 2013.

306 George Dura, "The EU and Moldova's Third Sector: Partners in Solving the Transnistria Conflict?", *MICROCON Policy Working Paper* (2010), pp. 1–34.

307 Anikó Hatoss, "Language, Faith and Identity. A Historical Insight into Discourses of Language Ideology and Planning by the Lutheran Church of Australia," *Australian Review of Applied Linguistics* 35 (2012), pp. 94–112.

Soviet Union helped the Transnistrian population to unite in the region not on the basis of nationality, but "Sovietness."

For almost 70 years, Transnistria, as a part of the Soviet Union, used communist symbols. After the collapse of the USSR and the self-proclamation of the TMR it had to create new state symbols for the new state. The easiest and the most attractive way was to borrow and transform the Soviet ones, creating a special new symbolism. The Soviet symbols were well recognized by the people and gave them a feeling of confidence and loyalty to the leadership that was using these symbols.

The Transnistrian authorities continued to use the flag of the MSSR as the state flag of the TMR. The coat of arms of the TMR is a remodeled version of the MSSR coat of arms. The only major change was the addition of waves, representing the Dniester River. Surprisingly, the hammer and sickle and the red star are retained in every Transnistrian state symbol. In May 2009 the Supreme Soviet of Transnistria proposed to use the Russian tricolor as the national flag of the region. This proposal was made in response to numerous requests by citizens who consider the Russian Federation "the successor of the USSR, the guarantor for settlement of the Transnistrian conflict, the country with which they strive to unite."[308] The Russian flag could have been seen alongside the republican flag on several administrative buildings in Tiraspol.

The coat of arms of the TMR is an image of two crossed hammers and sickles, symbolizing unity between workers and peasants. In the rays of the sun rising over the Dniester River, surrounded by a garland of ears of corn, fruits and grapes, are the words "Pridnestrovian Moldovan Republic" in Moldovan, Russian, and Ukrainian. At the top, there is a five-pointed red star with golden edges. The coat of arms shows the principle of multi-ethnicity and tolerance in the region.

Transnistrian state awards also have Soviet symbols. The "Order of the Republic," "The Order of Glory in Labour," and three other orders under the rubric, "For service to the homeland in the armed forces of Transnistria," all include the hammer and sickle and red stars.[309]

State symbols should reflect the history of the state, the relationship of the present with the past and focus on the future. In order to be effec-

---

308 Rossiyskiy tricolor stanet flagom Pridnestrovya [Russian Tricolor Will be the Flag of Transistria], *Kommersant* 4, May 2005. Accessible at: http://kommersant.ru/Doc-rm/1164262. Last retrieved 22 January 2013.

309 Ukaz ob utverzhdenii polozheniya o gosudarstvennyh nagradah PMR [Decree On State Awards of TMW]. Accessible at: http://zakon-pmr.com/DetailDoc.aspx?document=43991. Last retrieved 22 January 2013.

Figure 7.2 Coat of arms
of Transnistria.
Source: Wikimedia Commons.

tive, state symbols should be original, i.e., they should have their own design, not be copied from others. Hence, how effective are the current state symbols of the Republic of Moldova? If one takes into account the point of view of those who believe that the Moldovan people are an invention of Stalin, and that in fact Moldovans are Romanians, these state symbols are not appropriate since some of them were copied from Romanian ones (the flag, the coat of arms). For supporters of Moldova who believe that the current Republic of Moldova is the historic continuation of medieval Moldavia, the appropriateness of the national symbols is greater. It should be remembered that the current flag and coat of arms of the Republic of Moldova[310] were copied from Romanian samples[311] when the idea of unification with Romania was extremely popular. Apart from the Romanian-copied state symbols, we can see the flags of the European Union on several administrative buildings in the city of Chisinau, which would appear to show pro-European tendencies in the country and a desire to join the European Union.

A second wave of pro-Romanian orientation started in 2009 and continues to the present. On 13 July 2012 the Moldovan Government banned

---

310 *Natsionalniye simvoly Respubliky Moldova* [National Symbols of Moldova]. Accessible at: http://www.moldovenii.md/ru/section/721. Last retrieved 13 March 2013.

311 *Romania, an Overview. The National Symbols.* Accessible at: http://chisinau.mae.ro/en/romania/311. Last retrieved 13 March 2013.

the use of communist symbols for political purposes. The new law "On political and legal assessment of the totalitarian regime" was based on the work of the commission for studying the totalitarian regime. The Liberal Party (one of the parties of the ruling parliamentary coalition) was the initiator of this prohibition. The law primarily concerned the Communist Party of Moldova – the biggest opposition party – led by the former President of the Republic, Vladimir Voronin. The law condemns "the totalitarian communist regime in the Moldovan SSR, which committed crimes against humanity,"[312] and prohibits the use of communist symbols (the hammer and sickle were mentioned as examples) for political purposes. It is also forbidden to "promote totalitarian ideology."[313] In addition, a proposal for the prohibition of Soviet symbols in Chisinau was made by the local authorities, as was a ban on using the ribbons of Saint George, the symbol of Victory Day (9 May).[314] Additionally, the government is considering a draft law on the prohibition of all billboards and signs in the Russian language.[315]

The leadership of the two regions mobilizes the Soviet past for their own purposes in the cultural landscapes of cities: monuments, names of streets and civic places such as cinemas, shopping malls, cafés, squares, clubs, etc. The scriptwriter and journalist Joseph Reaney wrote in one guide: "Walking around Tiraspol is akin to wandering around Leningrad in its heyday, with stunning spectacles of the Cold War era on every corner. From severe-looking statues of Lenin and haphazardly-parked Soviet tanks to anti-imperialist graffiti and home-owned hammer and sickle flags; this is a city that is proud to be keeping the socialist end up."[316]

The fate of Soviet monuments after the collapse of the socialist system and communist regimes differs across the USSR successor states. Many

312 *Proiectul hotărîrii privind aprecierea politico-juridică a regimurilor totalitare în republica Moldova No. 1677* [The Draft Decision on the Political and Legal Assessment of Totalitarian Regimes in Moldova No. 1677]. Accessible at: http://www.parlament.md/ProcesulLegislativ/Proiectede-actelegislative/tabid/61/LegislativId/1319/Default.aspx. Last retrieved 30 January 2013.

313 Ibid.

314 "V Kishineve predlozhili zapretit georgiyevskiye lenty" [Ribbon of Saint George could be prohibited in Kishinev], *Lenta*, 30 April 2013. Accessible at: http://lenta.ru/news/2013/04/30/kishinev/. Last retrieved 4 May 2013.

315 "Parlament rassmotrit zakonoproekt zapreshiayushiiy reklamu i viveski na russkom yazike" [The Parliament will consider a law on the prohibition of usage of the Russian language on billboards and shop signs], *Panorama*. Accessible at: http://pan.md/news/Parlament-rassmo-trit-zakonoproekt-zapreshiayushiiy-reklamu-i-viveski-na-russkom-yazike/43342. Last retrieved 18 March 2014.

316 Joseph Reaney, "Travelling under Lenin's Watchful Eye," *Shoestring* 2 (2010), p. 18–19.

of the monuments of the Soviet era have become the objects of vandalism. Most of them were disassembled or destroyed by the authorities of the new republics; some were moved to other locations, often on the outskirts of cities, or to cemeteries, or special "Museums of the Soviet Occupation." Some of the monuments were sold to collectors or as scrap metal or were moved to Western Europe and the United States.

Soviet monuments, including statues of Lenin and Stalin, memorials to the October Revolution and its heroes, or to the Second World War and to the consolidation of the communist regime, or the history of the armed forces of the USSR and other socialist countries, are perceived differently in the two regions.

For example, the monument to Karl Marx and Friedrich Engels that was installed in 1976 near the parliament building of the Republic of Moldova in Chisinau was smashed with hammers by vandals in 1991. Then on 25 August 1991 it was disassembled by a decision of the Presidium of the Parliament of the Republic of Moldova.

Another case concerns the statue of Lenin that was built in October 1949 in the central square in front of the Chisinau Government House which was dismantled in 1991. Now it is located in the free economic zone "Moldexpo." Attempts to demolish the monument were made several times.

Even as old monuments are being dismantled in Moldova, new ones are appearing. A bust of the historian Nicolae Iorga (1871–1940) was unveiled on 31 August 1993 in the Stefan cel Mare Park. Nicolae Iorga was a Romanian historian, Byzantine scholar, literary critic, writer, politician, member of the Romanian Academy, and one of the founders of the National Democratic Party. In 1931–1932, he held the posts of prime minister and minister of national education. This demonstrates how Moldova is restoring the cultural heritage of the time when Bessarabia was part of Romania.

A new monument in Chisinau was built on the national holiday "Limba Noastra" on 31 August 2012. The bust of the first ruler of Romania was a gift from the Romanian District Council of Prahova.

On 27 June 2010, a memorial stone in memory of the victims of Soviet occupation and the totalitarian communist regime was installed at the place where the statue of Lenin had been located before 1991. In the same year, acting President Mihai Ghimpu declared 28 June as Memorial Day for victims of the Soviet occupation and the totalitarian communist regime. According to Ghimpu's speech, Bessarabia, the eastern part of the historical territory of Moldova, was invaded by Soviet troops on 28 June 1940.[317] Referring to the introduction of the new memorial day, Mihai Ghimpu stated that he considers this day a "black day" for Moldova, when the tragedy of the Moldovan people began.[318] However, the Constitutional Court of the Republic of Moldova on 12 July 2010 declared the decree unconstitutional.[319] These attempts to abandon the Soviet past have had an influence on the formation of self-image among the young people of Moldova.

On the other hand, monuments in Transnistria are closely linked to the history of Russia and the Soviet Union. On one Transnistrian tourism website it is written: "[…] we Transnistrians appreciate our history and unlike many of our fellows in the CIS, we are not fighting a war against it. We have not destroyed our monuments to Lenin and the great men of the Soviet era, and we have not renamed the streets honoring Soviet greatness. We recognize our history with pride, while still looking to the future."[320] This shows continuity from Soviet times and the tolerant attitude of the local population to the Soviet heritage.

This attitude is apparent in the cities of Transnistria. In the center of Tiraspol, in front of the building of the Supreme Soviet and the Government of Transnistria, a monument of Lenin, which was built in 1987, still stands. It is interesting that in Transnistria there are monuments not only of Soviet politicians and leaders but also of important figures from the Russian Empire.

The equestrian monument to Alexander Suvorov in Tiraspol (1979) is considered one of the best monuments of the general in the territory of the former USSR. Alexander Suvorov is considered to be the founder of Tiraspol. In accordance with his instructions, the fortress of Sredinnaja was established on the left bank of the Dniester River in 1792 to strengthen the new borders of the Russian Empire. From that fortress the city of Tiraspol was founded.

317 *V Moldove otmenen ukaz o Dne sovetskoy okkupatsii* [Decree on the Day of Soviet Occupation Is Abrogated in Moldova]. Accessible at: http://www.delfi.ua/news/daily/foreign/v-moldove-otmenen-ukaz-o-dne-sovetskoj-okkupacii.d?id=1076125. Last retrieved 5 July 2012.

318 Ibid.

319 *Konstitutsionniy sud Moldovy priznak nezakonnym ukaz o Dne sovetskoy okkupatsii* [The Constitutional Court of Moldova did not recognize the Decree on the Day of Soviet Occupation]. Accessible at: http://ru.tsn.ua/svit/konstitucionnyy-sud-moldovy-priznal-nezakonnym-ukaz-o-dne-sovetskoy-okkupacii.html, 6 July 2012.

320 *About Transnistria.* Accessible at: http://www.transnistria-tour.com/en/about-transnistria. Last retrieved 13 July 2012.

Figure 7.3 Lenin statue in front of the Transnistrian parliament building in Tiraspol, 2006.
Source: Guttorm Flatabø, Wikimedia Commons.

Economic Boom and the Growth of Cities

As a result of the economic circumstances prevailing during the Soviet and post-Soviet periods, the status of the cities changed. During the Soviet era, Transnistria was an important region for the party leadership. It became especially significant in 1950 when Leonid Brezhnev, on the recommendation of Nikita Khrushchev, held the post of First Secretary of the Central Committee of the MSSR Communist Party. Transnistria became a kind of training ground for future general secretaries of the communist party.

The Brezhnev period was characterized by increasing investment in industry, and new industries and large enterprises soon appeared in the region. The industrial units were generally concentrated in Transnistria: around Tiraspol and Bender, Ribnita, Dubăsari, and other cities. By 1959, the number of Transnistrian enterprises had reached 99. The number of people employed at these enterprises in the 1950s increased 2.4 times, and gross production 3.5 times.

In the period 1961–1990 new industries were created and developed in the MSSR, including electrical engineering, instrument making, energy and metallurgy, the production of hydraulic pumps, tractors, agricultural machines, and equipment for food processing, and light industry. The all-union model of production, in which raw materials were imported from and finished products exported to the other republics, was the main feature in the construction of the new enterprises.

Development projects in industrial zones on the outskirts of cities were widely implemented in the post-war period in the Soviet Union. Residents were to be accommodated in satellite-cities built around the new enterprises, and these would become the economic core for the development of the suburbs and the service sector, and would lessen environmental and transportation problems. The people of Transnistria thus experienced the realization of the main goals of the communist party.

In determining the main goals in building a communist society, the party was guided by Lenin's slogan: "Communism is Soviet power plus the electrification of the whole country."[321] The Dubossary hydroelectric power plant was the beginning of the large-scale electrification of Moldova. It went into operation in 1954 and was the first of its kind on the Dniester River. Its construction is linked to the revival of the city. The

---

321 *Materialy XXII syezda KPSS* [The Materials of XXII Congress of CPSU], Moscow: Gospolitizdat 1961, p. 368.

period from the 1950s to the 1970s was one of construction of new neigh-
borhoods, streets, industrial enterprises, kindergartens, schools, as well
as medical, cultural and sports institutions.

This rapid industrial development changed the appearance of cities.
Urban territory widened. In this way the center of Transnistria, Tiraspol,
grew. For instance, the Kirovsky district, the northernmost part of Tiraspol, is a relatively new area. It was built in the 1950s and 1960s. The
area is associated with industry because many of Tiraspol's large enterprises are located there. The city continued developing dynamically until
the late 1980s. High rates of industrial production and the construction
of new infrastructure promoted an influx of population, from Moldova,
from Russia, and the Ukraine.

The creation of the Moldovan GRES was accompanied by the simul-
taneous construction of Dnestrovsc. The town was founded in 1961. The
base of the power station was built first, and one year later a series of
multi-story housing blocks, shops, a hair salon and other day-to-day services opened. In addition, schools and a "House of Culture" appeared in
the town.

Although the new districts were not always built in line with technical norms and safety standards, for the inhabitants of Transnistria they
meant something special: to get a job, to receive an apartment from the
state, to work at an enterprise highly important at the all-union level.
It is clear that, in Transnistria, the formulated goals of the party were
embodied in real life.

The period from the 1950s to the 1980s in the MSSR was characterized by strong positive demographic trends. The population grew quickly due to a high birth rate, a relatively low mortality rate, and an excep-
tionally large positive migratory balance that prevailed in the region.
Indeed, a natural increase in Moldovan SSR was higher than in the three
Baltic republics combined. Favorable weather conditions, a tolerant mul-
tinational composition of the population, an advantageous geographical
position, and a high level of development within the economic complex
of the USSR all influenced the attractiveness of migration to the zone
during the pre-conflict period.

By the late 1980s Transnistria was an urbanized and highly industrial-
ized region. Well-developed industrial and agricultural sectors were the
basis of its economy. Transnistria, with a population composed of 0.25%
from the USSR and 17% from the MSSR, produced approximately 1% of
the gross domestic product of the USSR (including 2% of its agricultural
production) and about 35% of the gross national product of the MSSR

(including 90% of its electricity, 56% of consumer goods, and one-third of its agricultural products).[322] The formation of the industrial structure of the Transnistrian economy was determined by environmental conditions (climate, fertile soil), favorable for the development of agriculture.

The regional advantages of Transnistria were evident: transport accessibility (railway, highways, and the Dniester River), the availability of water resources, low seismic activity, proximity to the ports of Odessa and Mariupol (the Donetsk region) and to the Dnieper region, which was rich in metal and coal. Some 100 enterprises in machine-building, light industry, building materials, furniture, microbiology, etc., were located in the Transnistrian part of the MSSR.[323] However, the region lacked fuel, energy and raw material resources. Of minerals important for industry, only limestone, clay and sand were present.

Such economic indicators and the special status of Transnistria (i.e., partly autonomous in the context of the USSR) could be seen as influencing attitudes in the future Pridnestrovian Republic in terms of nationalism and the influence of the Moldovan Central Committee. Subsidized by Moscow during the Soviet years, Transnistria is still tied to Russia, despite the collapse of the USSR. Many Transnistrian enterprises partly or completely belong to Russian owners. In 2003 the plant "Pribor" was purchased by the Moscow machine-building production enterprise "Salyut." This sale led to the appearance of the first Russian Federation state property in the territory of Transnistria.[324] In 2005 the Kuchurgan power station was privatized and then became part of the Russian group Inter RAOUES.[325] Since 2009, Moldavskaya GRES has been the main supplier of electricity to Moldova. We can say that continuity and the orderly operation of business are evident in the region.

Today the Soviet Red star and the star of Sheriff[326] are both symbols of Transnistria. The first symbol is taken from the USSR and signifies

322 Vladislav Grosul, *Istoriya Pridnestrovskoy Moldavskoy Respubliky* [The History of TMR], Tiraspol: RIOPGU 2000, p. 327.

323 Center for Strategic Studies and Reforms. *Evolutsiya Ekonomiky Pridnestrovya: kriticheskaya otsenka* [Evolution of the Transnistrian Economy: Critical Assessment]. Accessible at: http://www.cisr-md.org/pdf/0111%20Transnistria_Report_En_Final%20RUS.pdf. Last retrieved 5 April 2013.

324 Official website of Bender City. Accessible at: http://bendery.su/Ekonomika/pribor.html. Last retrieved 9 April 2013.

325 INTER RAO official website. Accessible at: http://www.interrao.ru/en/company/structure/. Last retrieved 9 April 2013.

326 The largest private Transnistrian company established in 1993, which owns supermarkets, gas stations, football stadiums, mobile telephone, and internet connections.

the high industrial potential of the Soviet years. The second symbolizes the business model of the West, a Europeanized image of the future of the region.

Changing Street Names

Changing the names of streets is also crucial in the process of forming the identity of a people. Mia Swart affirms that "since memory is closely connected to the identity symbolized by a name, those who cannot be named cannot be remembered. To retrieve a name is to rescue a person from oblivion."[327]

Commemorative street names are a common feature of modern political culture, but this custom is not obligatory. Streets can have alphanumeric names, like 5th Avenue and 62nd Street in New York, which take their names from the practical function of denoting a location. "Commemorative street names, together with commemorative monuments and heritage museums, not only represent a particular version of history but are also participants in the ongoing cultural production of a shared past."[328]

The naming of streets is an administrative and political act, the responsibility of the authorities, and expresses their power. One of the functions of street-naming is the construction of a politicized version of history which is "prone to manipulation and should therefore be viewed with caution."[329] The Soviet leadership made extensive use of street names, commemorating political figures such as Vladimir Lenin. "The renaming of streets is a conventional manifestation of a stage of liminal transition in political history, when the need of the new regime for legitimacy and self-presentation is especially high; it is an act of political propaganda with immense proclamative value and public resonance."[330]

The Soviet period likewise had its de-commemorations. After the death of Stalin, the dismantling of his personality cult began in the USSR. These actions were taken to eliminate the symbolic presence of party leaders from the public realm. Thus, what happened in the union

---

327 Mia Swart, "Name Changes as Symbolic Reparation after Transition: the Examples of Germany and South Africa," *German Law Journal* 9, no. 2 (2008), pp. 105–120.
328 Maoz Azaryahu, "The Power of Commemorative Street Names," *Environment and Planning D: Society and Space* 14 (1996), pp. 311–330.
329 Swart 2008, p. 106.
330 Azaryahu 1996, p. 318.

republics after the collapse of the USSR (the renaming of streets, the destruction of monuments from the communist regime) was a typical process. The names of many streets in Chisinau were changed under the pro-Romanian policy. The attempt to rename the streets associated with the Soviet period could be seen as an intention to interpret history in a different way.

In 1970 one of the new streets in Chisinau was named Belski Street (Strada Beliski) in honor of the hero of the Soviet Union and honorary citizen of the city, Colonel Alexei Belski (1914–1970), under whose command Soviet troops in 1944 broke through to the center of the city and hoisted the red flag over one of the collapsed buildings in Chisinau. In 1991, the street was renamed in honor of Alexandru Ioan Cuza-Vodă, the prince who in 1859 united part of Moldavia over the Prut River (which was not part of the Russian Empire) and Wallachia under the suzerainty of Turkey. He called the new territorial union Romania. Under his rule the Romanian language adopted a Latin-based alphabet. This renaming of the street underlined the desire of the Moldovan authorities to introduce their language policy and to consolidate their identity in the public sphere. However, after 21 years, and numerous street rallies, the original name Belski Street was restored.

Pushkin Street (Strada Puşkin) is a street in the municipality of Chisinau and is one of the main streets in the city center. Pushkin Street was known as Episcopal Street (Arhierejskaja ulitsa) from 1834 to 1874. In 1874 the street was renamed Province Street (Gubernskaja Ulitsa) in honor of Bessarabia receiving the status of province (guberniya) of the Russian Empire in 1873. It retained this name until 1899 when the street was renamed again, this time in honor of the great Russian poet Alexander Pushkin, and until 1918 it was called Pushkin Street. During Romanian rule in Bessarabia in the interwar period, the street carried the name of King Charles I.[331]

In 2009 a fierce dispute broke out over the renaming of Pushkin Street in honor of Grigore Vieru, a Moldovan poet and supporter of the unification of Romania and Moldova who was killed in a car accident. The idea of renaming one of the central streets of the city in honor of Vieru was proposed by the Moldovan composer Eugen Doga, who later commented in the press that he had not specified which street should be renamed.[332] In the end, the Mayor of Chisinau, Dorin Chirtoaca, took

---

331 The title existed until 1944 when it again reverted to Pushkin Street.

332 *Ulitsa Pushkina stanet ulitsey Vieru?* [Will Pushkin Street Become Vieru Street?]. Accessible at: http://baza.md/index.php?newsid=395. Last retrieved 8 July 2012.

Figure 7.4 Building on Ştefan cel Mare avenue 132 in Chişinău, 2015.
Source: Gikü, Wikimedia Commons.

the initiative and on 22 February 2010 the name of Grigore Vieru was officially awarded to part of Renaşterii Avenue and Pushkin Street retained
its name.

Another instance was the renaming of the Boulevard Stefan cel Mare
(Prince of Moldavia between 1457 and 1504), the main street in Chisinau. In the early nineteenth century it was called Millionaya Street (ulitsa Milionnaja). In the 1840s it was renamed Moscow Street. This name
continued until 1877 when it became Alexander Street and remained so
until 1924. From 1924 until 1944, the period when Bessarabia was part
of Romania, the street was divided into two parts: one retained the name
Alexander Street, and the second took the name of the Boulevard of
King Carol II. In 1944 it became known as Lenin Street, and from 1952
to 1990 as Lenin Avenue. As can be seen, most of the time this street bore
names connected with the Russian Empire or with the Soviet Union, and
only in 1991 did the street receive a new identity.

The Boulevard of the Soviet Army (Bul'var Sovetskoy Armii) was
built in the 1970s in Chisinau. The street was declared open on the 30th
anniversary of the liberation of Moldova in 1944. After a declaration of
independence by Moldova, the street was renamed Traian Boulevard
(Bulevardul Traian) in honor of the Roman emperor Trajan who conquered the land of Dacia in the early years of the second century AD.

Figure 7.5 "We want union with Romania/Russia" graffiti, 2013.
Source: Simiprof, Wikimedia Commons.

Peace Avenue (Prospekt Mira) was built in the second half of the 1960s in Chisinau, and was declared to be one of the main roads of the city. In the late 1980s, the housing estate "Gate City" was built on the road leading to the city's airport. After 1990, the street was renamed Dacia Avenue (Bulevardul Dacia) in honor of the people of Dacia, from whom, as is commonly believed, the Moldovans descended. The name change in this case is especially significant since this is the street one follows when entering the city from the airport.

Alba Iulia Street (Strada Alba-Iulia) is also one of the many renamed streets in Chisinau. It was originally called Buiucani Street, and was later renamed Engels Street in honor of one of the founders of Marxism, Friedrich Engels. From 1970 to 1990 it was called Engels Avenue (Prospekt Engelsa). Finally, in 1990 it was named after the Romanian town Alba Iulia.

Decebal Boulevard (Bulevardul Decebal) also has a long history. The street was built in the late nineteenth century and was named Bachojskaya Road. Until the 1950s it passed through the suburbs of Chisinau, where gardens and vineyards were located. After the liberation of Moldova from Romanian occupation and reconstruction of the area, the road was named Lvov Street. From the end of the 1960s it was called Timoshenko Street in honour of Semyon Timoshenko, Marshal of the USSR. In 1989 the street acquired a new name – Decebal Boulevard. Decebalus (originally called Diurpaneus) was the last ruler, military leader, and high priest of Dacia (87–106 AD).

In contrast, the names of the streets in Transnistria remained largely unchanged. 25th October Street (Ulitsa 25-go Octyabrya) is one of the main roads in the Transnistrian capital of Tiraspol. Before the 1880s, it was the postal road and its name was accordingly Post Street (Pochtovaya ulitsa). Later, the street was called *Pokrovskaya* after the Pokrov Church, which was founded in 1798 and demolished in 1931. The street was renamed "25th October Street" in 1921, the name it retains today.

The longest street in Tiraspol is dedicated to Karl Liebknecht, the leader of the German and international labor and socialist movement, and one of the founders of the German Communist Party in 1918. Earlier, it had been called Trade Street (ulitsa Remeslennaja). It is noteworthy that even Lenin Street still exists in Tiraspol.

Streets in Transnistria, however, do not have only Soviet names. There is in fact a mixture of names from the Russian Empire and the Soviet epoch: Chekhov Street, Tolstoy Street, Gogol Street, Kutuzov Street, Odessa Street, Suvorov Street, Cantemir Street, etc.

Other public places also underwent name changes. The Park Ştefan cel Mare is located in the heart of Chisinau. It was created in 1818, on the initiative of the wife of the governor of Bessarabia, Aleksej Bakhmetev. Originally, it had no name and was simply called City Garden, although the townspeople informally referred to it as Alexandrovskij Park. In 1885, a bronze bust of the Russian poet Alexander Pushkin was put in the middle of the park. In Soviet times the park was known as Pushkin Park. After the collapse of the Soviet Union it was renamed Ştefan cel Mare Park.

Conclusion

We can see that names play a major role in the creation of a positive or negative sense of place. "Names change because society changes."[333] There are many examples throughout history when authorities changed

---

333 Sylvain Guyot – Cecil Seethal, "Identity of Place, Places of Identities, Change of Place Names in Post-Apartheid South Africa," *The South African Geographical Journal* 89, no. 1 (2007), pp. 55–63.

the names of public places. For instance, during the French Revolution the names of streets were used for purposes of political representation. Instead of the statue of Louis XV in Paris a huge monument of Liberty was erected in 1792, and the square where it was located was renamed Place de la Revolution, today the Place de la Concorde. "The practice of commemoration by choosing and changing street and square names in Paris became an important component of French political symbolism."[334]

We have seen how the authorities in Transnistria exploited the Soviet past to justify the legitimacy of their power and to shape how people viewed the world by using Soviet symbols, holidays and customs. The Soviet past was artfully mined for images, symbols and models to facilitate the creation of an idealized history and to initiate the idea of a Transnistrian nation.[335] In contrast, the authorities of the Republic of

Figure 7.6 Welcome sign at the east end of Tiraspol, 2013.
Source: Nixalsverdrus, Wikimedia Commons.

---

334 Swart 2008, p. 114.
335 Stela Suhan – Natalia Cojocaru, "Stratagems in the Construction of the Transnistrian Identity," *Psihologia socială* 15 (2006), pp. 119–134, here p. 126.

Moldova excluded the Soviet legacy and fashioned other symbols and images to influence people's perception of reality and likewise that of future generations.

The Soviet past itself enabled the creation of an idealized history and the idea of a Transnistrian nation.[336] A nostalgia for Soviet ideology exists and has helped to form a Soviet political identity as an alternative to an ethnic one. In contrast, Moldova eschews Soviet symbolism in order to reinforce their own national idea of statehood.

Despite the different outlooks of Moldovan citizens on either side of the Dniester River, there are similarities as well. Identity in Moldova and Transnistria, based on linguistic and ideological controversy, has a clearly transitional nature. It has still not completely formed and a certain time frame must elapse before it either solidifies or, alternatively, becomes weaker.

336 Ibid.

About the Authors

Jaroslav Ira graduated in 2005 with a degree in History and Political Science at Charles University in Prague, where he also obtained his PhD in 2013 with the thesis *Local and National Identity in Historical Monographs on Bohemian, Moravian, and Galician Towns (1860–1900)*. At present, he is lecturer at the Faculty of Arts (Institute of World History), and at the CEVRO Institute. He specializes in the modern history of East-Central Europe, concentrating in particular on the formations and intersections of local, regional, national, European, urban and civic identities, urban studies, social uses of the past, and theoretical and methodological questions of historiography.

Jiří Janáč is a lecturer at the Seminar of General and Comparative History, Institute of World History at the Faculty of Arts and post-doc researcher at the Institute for Contemporary History of the Czech Academy of Science. Jiří has defended his PhD thesis *cum Laude* at the Eindhoven University of Technology, Eindhoven, the Netherlands. He was attached to the Czech National Heritage Institute 2005–2007. His research interests focus on the social and cultural history of technology in 20th century Europe. He is the author of *"European Coasts of Bohemia Negotiating the Danube-Oder-Elbe Canal in a Troubled Twentieth Century"*, Amsterdam 2012.

Natallia Linitskaya is a doctoral student at the Institute of World History at the Faculty of Arts and a holder of 2015 Karen Johnson Freeze Fellowship. She took her master's degree from Charles University in Prague. She specializes in comparative urban history.

ana **Nikolovska** took her master's degree from TEMA master's program which she carried in Prague, Budapest and Paris from Charles University in Prague.

Olga Niutenko took her master's degree in Political Sciences from CEU in Budapest and from TEMA master's program which she carried in Prague and Catania.

Nari Shelekpayev is a doctoral student at Université de Montréal. He took his master's degree from Paris1-Sorbonne in Law, and from TEMA master's program which he carried in Prague, Catania and Paris. He specializes in comparative urban history. He published several articles on capital cities in non-European states.